# AN INVITATION TO ACTION

# LUTHERAN-REFORMED DIALOGUE III (1981–1983)

---

## PARTICIPATING CHURCHES

*Lutheran Churches*

The Association of Evangelical Lutheran Churches (AELC)

The American Lutheran Church (ALC)

Lutheran Church in America (LCA)

The Lutheran Church—Missouri Synod (LCMS)

*Reformed Churches*

The Reformed Church in America (RCA)

The Presbyterian Church (U.S.A.) (PC[U.S.A.])

The Cumberland Presbyterian Church

The United Church of Christ (UCC)

# FINAL REPORT

Series I: 1962–1966
(U.S.A. National Committee
of the Lutheran World Federation
and the North American Area of the
World Alliance of Reformed Churches)

Series II: 1972–1974
(Division of Theological Studies
of the Lutheran Council in the U.S.A.
and the North American Area Council of the
World Alliance of Reformed Churches)

THE LUTHERAN-REFORMED DIALOGUE
SERIES III, 1981–1983

---

# AN INVITATION TO ACTION

*A Study of Ministry, Sacraments, and Recognition*

James E. Andrews and
Joseph A. Burgess, Editors

FORTRESS PRESS PHILADELPHIA

This book is the Final Report of the Lutheran-Reformed Dialogue III (1981–1983) held under the auspices of the Division of Theological Studies of the Lutheran Council in the U.S.A. and the Caribbean and North American Area Council of the World Alliance of Reformed Churches.



---

Library of Congress Catalog Card Number:
84–47885

ISBN 0–8006–1818–1

---

1109B84 Printed in the United States of America 1–1818

# CONTENTS

# FOREWORD

This new series of dialogue has had the advantage of a new ecumenical climate. Our churches have been in the intervening years more and more deeply engaged in conversation within our confessional families and across confessional lines. We were able very quickly to find common faith, common history, common language, and common concerns for the future. Some of the Lutheran and some of the Reformed churches were simultaneously engaged in negotiating intra-confessional unions. We had a sense of urgency about a common mission confronting all our churches.

We began by studying carefully the reports of the first two series of the Lutheran-Reformed dialogue in America, the Leuenberg Agreement of the Lutheran and Reformed churches in Europe, and the reports of the bilateral discussions which each of our confessional families has had with other confessional bodies. We felt that excellent studies had already provided a solid foundation for our work. What seemed most lacking was a study of ministry reflecting our churches' current concerns. Therefore several of our twice-yearly sessions were devoted to papers on this topic. In our final sessions, concluding in October 1983, we developed the common statements and recommendations printed in the first section of this volume. We then assembled the documentary material found in the appendixes in order to facilitate the study of our statements by a wide spectrum of church members.

We present this report and study document to our churches with gratitude for the experience of Christian unity which we have had but also with an urgent appeal that a broad representation of our members become involved together in that ongoing common study, worship, and mission to which we believe the Holy Spirit is calling us today.

Jane D. Douglass and
Edward K. Perry, *Co-chairpersons*

# ACKNOWLEDGEMENTS

Quotations from *Baptism, Eucharist and Ministry* (Geneva: World Council of Churches, 1982) are reprinted by permission of the Faith and Order Commission of the World Council of Churches.

Chapter 1, The Government, from *The Book of Church Order* (New York: Reformed Church Press, 1982 ed.), pp. 16–17, is reprinted by permission of the Reformed Church in America.

Quotations from *The Book of Concord,* trans. and ed. Theodore G. Tappert (Philadelphia: Fortress Press, 1981), are reprinted by permission of the publisher.

Quotations from *The Book of Confessions* and *The Book of Order* of the *Constitution of the Presbyterian Church* (New York and Atlanta: Offices of the General Synod, 1981) are reprinted by permission of the Stated Clerk of the General Assembly of the Presbyterian Church (U.S.A.).

The essay "Church and Ministry" by Warren A. Quanbeck, originally presented at the consultation of the Division of Theological Studies of the Lutheran Council in the U.S.A. held 20–21 September 1971 in Chicago, is used by permission of Mrs. Warren A. Quanbeck.

The quotation from the *Confession of Faith and Government* of the Cumberland Presbyterian Church, p. iv, is reprinted by permission of the General Assembly of the Cumberland Presbyterian Church.

The quotation from *Ecumenical Relations of the Lutheran World Federation: Report of the Working Group on the Interrelations Between the Various Bilateral Dialogues* (Geneva: Lutheran World Federation, 1977), pp. 100–101, is reprinted by permission of the publisher.

Quotations from *Essays on the Lord's Supper,* trans. J. G. Davies (Atlanta: John Knox Press, 1958) are reprinted by permission of the publisher.

The Leuenberg Agreement (*Lutheran World* 20 [1973]:347–53) is reprinted by permission of the publisher.

Quotations from the *Lutheran-Episcopal Dialogue: Report and Recommendations,* published by Forward Movement Publications, 412 Sycamore St., Cincinnati, Ohio 45202, are reprinted by permission of the publisher.

Appendix 1 of this volume and other quotations are reprinted by permission from *Marburg Revisited,* ed. Paul C. Empie and James I. McCord, copyright © 1966 by Augsburg Publishing House.

The quotation from *Principles of Lutheran Theology* by Carl E. Braaten (Philadelphia: Fortress Press, 1983), pp. 94–95, is reprinted by permission of the publisher.

The quotation from *The Unity of the Church: Requirements and Structure* by Gassman and Meyer (Stuttgart: Lutheran World Federation, 1983), p. 14, is reprinted by permission of the publisher.

# ABBREVIATIONS

| | |
|---|---|
| AELC | Association of Evangelical Lutheran Churches |
| ALC | The American Lutheran Church |
| Ap | Apology of the Augsburg Confession |
| *BC* | *Book of Confessions* |
| *BCO* | *Book of Church Order* |
| BelC | Belgic Confession |
| *BEM* | *Baptism, Eucharist and Ministry* |
| *BkC* | *Book of Concord*, tr. and ed. T. Tappert (Philadelphia: Fortress Press, 1959) |
| *BO* | *Book of Order* |
| C'67 | Confession of 1967 |
| Cambridge Platform | Cambridge Platform of 1648, see Williston Walker, ed., *The Creeds and Platforms of Congregationalism* (Boston: Pilgrim Press, 1960) |
| CA | Augsburg Confession |
| FC SD | Formula of Concord, Solid Declaration |
| HCat | Heidelberg Catechism |
| LA | Leuenberg Agreement |
| *LBW* | *Lutheran Book of Worship* |
| LC | Large Catechism |
| LCA | Lutheran Church in America |
| LCMS | The Lutheran Church—Missouri Synod |
| LCUSA | Lutheran Council in the U.S.A. |
| LED | Lutheran-Episcopal Dialogue |
| LR | Lutheran-Reformed |
| LWF | Lutheran World Federation |
| PC(U.S.A.) | Presbyterian Church (U.S.A.) |
| PCUS | Presbyterian Church in the United States |
| RCA | Reformed Church in America |
| SA | Smalcald Articles |
| SC | Small Catechism |
| ScotsC | Scots Confession |
| II HC | Second Helvetic Confession |
| UCC | United Church of Christ |
| UPCUSA | United Presbyterian Church in the U.S.A. |
| WARC | World Alliance of Reformed Churches |
| WC | Westminster Confession |

# PARTICIPANTS

**LUTHERAN:**

*Dr. Keith Bridston* (ALC)
Theological Consultant to the General Secretariat of the World Council of Churches
New York, New York

*Rev. George Dolak* (LCMS)
Pastor
St. John Evangelical Lutheran Church
Brackenridge, Pennsylvania

*Dr. Robert H. Fischer* (LCA)
Professor of Church History
Lutheran School of Theology at Chicago, Illinois

*Dr. Edward K. Perry** (LCA)
Bishop
Upper New York Synod
Lutheran Church in America
Syracuse, New York

*Dr. Karl Reko* (AELC)
Assistant Professor in the Practical Theology Department
Christ Seminary—Seminex
St. Louis, Missouri

*Dr. William G. Rusch* (LCA)**
Director, Ecumenical Relations
Lutheran Church in America
New York, New York

*Dr. Howard W. Tepker* (LCMS)
Dean
Concordia Theological Seminary
Fort Wayne, Indiana

*Dr. Walter R. Wietzke* (ALC)
Director
Division for Theological Education and Ministry
The American Lutheran Church
Minneapolis, Minnesota

*Dr. Joseph A. Burgess* (Staff)
Executive Director
Division of Theological Studies
Lutheran Council in the U.S.A.
New York, New York

*Co-chairpersons
**Division of Theological Studies standing committee representative

# PARTICIPANTS

REFORMED:

*Dr. E. Colvin Baird* (Cumberland Presbyterian Church)
President
Memphis Theological Seminary
Memphis, Tennessee

*Dr. Jane D. Douglass** (PC[U.S.A.])
Professor of Church History
School of Theology at Claremont, California

*Dr. Paul Fries* (RCA)
Associate Professor of Theology and Ministry
New Brunswick Theological Seminary
New Brunswick, New Jersey

*Dr. Aurelia T. Fule* (PC[U.S.A.])
The Program Agency
The United Presbyterian Church
New York, New York

*Dr. Frederick Herzog* (UCC)
Professor
The Divinity School
Duke University
Durham, North Carolina

*Dr. Eugene March* (PC[U.S.A.])
Professor of Old Testament
Louisville Presbyterian Theological Seminary
Louisville, Kentucky

*Dr. Keith Nickle* (PC[U.S.A.])
Pastor
First Presbyterian Church
Jefferson City, Tennessee

*Dr. James E. Andrews* (Staff)
Interim Co-Stated Clerk
Presbyterian Church (U.S.A.)
Atlanta, Georgia

*Co-chairpersons

# PARTICIPATING CHURCHES

LUTHERAN CHURCHES

*The Association of Evangelical Lutheran Churches (AELC)* was formed in 1976 by a group which had been in long controversy with The Lutheran Church—Missouri Synod (LCMS). Their aim has been to continue to live for the causes which led them to leave the LCMS. They are members of those groups forming a new Lutheran church to begin in 1988. As with most Lutheran churches they subscribe to the Lutheran Confessions in the *Book of Concord.*

*The American Lutheran Church (ALC)* was begun in 1960 as a merger of the Norwegians—Evangelical Lutheran Church, the Germans—the old ALC, and the Danes—the United Evangelical Lutheran Church. In 1963 the Norwegians who had formed the Lutheran Free Church early in the century also joined the ALC. The ALC subscribes to the Lutheran Confessions in the *Book of Concord* and is part of the movement which is to form a new Lutheran church in 1988.

*The Lutheran Church in America (LCA)* was formed in 1962 as a merger of the Swedish Lutherans—Augustana Synod, the Finnish Lutherans—Suomi Synod, the Danes—American Evangelical Lutheran Church (AELC), and the United Lutheran Church in America (ULCA). The ULCA came largely out of German background, although others, such as the Slovak, were also part of its tradition. The LCA holds to the Lutheran Confessions in the *Book of Concord* and is part of the group forming a new Lutheran church in 1988.

*The Lutheran Church—Missouri Synod (LCMS)* began in 1839 when Saxon immigrants came to the United States. They remain a unified group with strong emphasis on the Lutheran Confessions and are not part of the group forming a new Lutheran church in 1988.

REFORMED CHURCHES

*The Reformed Church in America,* founded in 1628, grows out of the Reformed Church of the Netherlands. As doctrinal standards it holds the Belgic Confession of Faith, the Heidelberg Catechism with its Compendium, and the Canons of the Synod of Dort. In polity its *Book of Church Order* follows the traditional presbyterian form of government. There are three offices with governmental functions: the minister of the word, the elder, and the deacon. The office of professor of theology serves the church seminaries in ministerial training.

*The Presbyterian Church (U.S.A.)* was formed in June 1983 as a reunion of a church which had divided in the Civil War period. At the time the Lutheran-Reformed Dialogue III began, this church was represented by two bodies, the Presbyterian Church in the United States and the United Presbyterian Church in the U.S.A., heirs of the English-speaking Calvinistic tradition which named itself "presbyterian" after its form of government by elders and used the Westminster Confession as its doctrinal standard. The Presbyterian Church in the United States continued to use the Westminster Confession alone as its confessional standard. The United Presbyterian Church in the U.S.A. did so until 1967, when it adopted a *Book of Confessions* consisting of the Nicene Creed, the Apostles' Creed, the Scots' Confession, the Heidelberg Catechism, the Second Helvetic Confession, the Westminster Confession of Faith, the Shorter Catechism, the Theological Declaration of Barmen, and the Confession of 1967. The reunited church has declared that "The confessional documents of the two preceding Churches shall be the confessional documents of the reunited Church" (*Plan for Reunion* 3.1; see new *Book of Order* G–2.0). Both the former churches followed traditional presbyterian polity, and their Books of Order have remained very similar. The reunited church continues to ordain pastors, elders, and deacons.

*The Cumberland Presbyterian Church* was organized within the context of the revival movement in the early part of the nineteenth century. Its founders were Presbyterian ministers who could no longer accept the Westminster Confession's view of election and reprobation. Its Confession of faith, therefore, is a revision of the Westminster Confession which has eliminated the teaching of "universal foreordination and its legitimate sequences, unconditional election and reprobation, limited atonement, and divine influence correspondingly circumscribed" (Preface to *Confession of Faith and Government*, p. iv). A new Confession of faith has been prepared jointly with the Second Cumberland Presbyterian Church and is now in process of ratification by presbyteries after approval by the General Assemblies of the two churches. The church is governed in the presbyterian tradition and ordains pastors, elders, and deacons.

*The United Church of Christ,* founded in 1957, is distinctive from those listed above. It is shaped by the model of organic union merging the confessional and the convenantal traditions. After more than twenty-five years, it still finds itself in the process of being a "uniting church" (*Constitution,* 33) even in its own life as a denomination. Bringing together congregations from both the North American Congregational Christian traditions and from the former Evangelical and Reformed Church of continental background, this church has Calvinist roots on both sides of its family lineage, and it desires to keep alive its family ties. Therefore it participates in the Reformed community as well as in other groups with which it has historic ties. Since 1980 it is related to Lutheran traditions also through full communion with the Evangelical Church of the Union in the German Democratic Republic and the Federal German Republic. "It claims as its own the faith of the historic Church expressed in the ancient creeds and reclaimed in the basic insights of the Protestant Reformers. It affirms the responsibility of the Church in each generation to make this faith its own in reality of worship, in honesty of thought and expression, and in purity of heart before God" (*Constitution,* 2). Acceptance of particular historic creeds (for example, in ordination) is not an explicit point of church bylaws. It differs from the traditional Reformed pattern in that it roots the Confession in Jesus Christ, Son of God and Savior, in the local church covenant as the locus of authority of faith, and its polity is not presbyterian. The United Church of Christ does share many other characteristics of Reformed churches, however, including representative governance, a deep ecumenical commitment, a strong sense of mission, and a great concern for reform and ongoing renewal in the church as well as a live social witness. It ordains pastors.

All of these Reformed churches, except the Cumberland Presbyterian Church, are members of the World Alliance of Reformed Churches, the National Council of Churches, and the World Council of Churches.

# AN INVITATION TO ACTION

## INTRODUCTION

This common statement and urgent invitation for action is addressed to the Lutheran and Reformed churches[1] of the United States which appointed us as official representatives for the third round of theological dialogue between our confessional families.

Our common statement is the product of two years of study and explicitly builds on the earlier work of the theologians of our churches. The first round of Lutheran-Reformed dialogue, which concluded in 1966, was also the first bilateral theological conversation authorized by our churches. Those Lutheran-Reformed conversations thus began a new era in ecumenism.

Both the first and second rounds of dialogue invited our respective churches to take specific positive actions[2] to encourage our two traditions of the continental Reformation to recognize significant theological convergence and to participate in specific common activities. We regret that our respective churches did not do so as early as 1966.

We affirm that it is now an appropriate time for our churches to take positive action.

1. "For God so loved the world . . . "

1.1 God enters history in the Son and the Spirit to save and liberate the world from the bondage of sin and death. Sin is evidenced in our alienation from God and from one another, in the misuse and scarring of the goodness of creation and in injustice all around us. "The whole creation groans and travails in pain together until now" (Rom. 8:22). In Christ, God robs death of its power over creation. Through the resurrection God reverses the decay of all things. God's own mission in the world among all peoples goes on constantly. The existence of the ongoing people of God offers hope in our culture gripped alternately by arrogant self-sufficiency and despair.

1.2 This mission of God in such a world addresses churches of common faith. Today there is a new urgency to unite in common proclamation of the gospel, witnessing to the kingdom of God and its justice (Matt. 6:33). Humankind seems bent upon bringing the end of the world upon itself and all creatures of God by nuclear holocaust. Our churches are already enlisted in a common mission: participation in God's preservation of the world, God's struggle for justice and peace, and evangelization.

1.3 The people of our churches live in the same communities, work in the same buildings, perform the same tasks, suffer the same pains, celebrate the same joys, and are sustained by the same gospel.

1.4 Each of our churches independently has addressed issues common to our local communities, our nation, and the world, such as: nuclear armament, peace, justice for the poor of our country and the world, prison reform, sex, marriage, and the family, economic justice, the yokes of race and class, ecology, and the advocacy of all persons denied their right to achieve their potential.

1.5 Our churches in varying degrees already cooperate with each other locally, nationally, and internationally in addressing the urgent needs of our world and in confessing God's work among us.

1.6 Because our churches are engaged in a consideration of the document on *Baptism, Eucharist and Ministry* developed within the World Council of Churches, we are obligated to explore again the heritage of ministry, sacraments, and mission we share as churches shaped by the Reformation of the sixteenth century.

1.7 Because we have commonality in our theological reflections and our social setting in spite of our separation, God's mission presses us on to a more visible unity rooted in God's word and sacraments.

1.8 Because God makes us all members of the holy catholic church by baptism, our churches are compelled to work together officially toward full communion in each other's baptism, Holy Communion,[3] and ministry.

1.9 Our unity in word and sacraments will be one additional step for our churches as we pray for and accept the unity Christ has given us, so that the world might believe and be re-created.

2. Our unity in Christ compels us to claim our strong affinities in doctrine and practice. Both Lutheran and Reformed traditions:

a. Affirm themselves a living part of the church catholic.
b. Confess the Nicene and Apostles' Creeds.[4]
c. Affirm the doctrine of justification by faith as fundamental.[5]
d. Affirm the unique and final authority of Holy Scriptures in the church.[6]
e. Affirm the real presence of Christ in the Lord's Supper.[7]
f. Affirm the priesthood of all believers and have interpreted this as our servanthood to God and our service to the world.[8]

g. Affirm the vocation of all the baptized, which is service (ministry) in every aspect of their lives in their care of God's world.[9]
h. Affirm that they are in faithful succession in the apostolic Tradition and that faithful succession in this Tradition is all that is necessary for mutual recognition as part of the church catholic.[10]
i. Share a common definition of a church in the apostolic Tradition: a community where the word is rightly preached and the sacraments rightly administered.[11]
j. Identify a ministry of word and sacrament as instituted by God.[12]
k. Ordain once to a ministry of word and sacrament, and the functions of such persons are identical.
l. Understand that ordination is to the ministry of the church catholic.[13] Such ordinations in both traditions have usually been by presbyters.[14]
m. Have granted the appropriateness under some circumstances of one ordained person exercising *episkopē*, oversight (under a variety of titles including that of bishop), but both traditions have ordinarily exercised the function of *episkopē* collegially through such structures as presbyteries and synods.
n. Affirm that the church always must be open to further growth and reformation. Both traditions have been willing to be self-critical. Both traditions have become increasingly open to a historical-critical understanding of the history of the church and of their respective traditions within the apostolic Tradition.[15]

3. Shared appreciation for the gifts and unique heritage of each of our traditions drives us to affirmation of our unity in Christ.

3.1 Our traditions, both rooted in the same reforming movement of the sixteenth century, have been strongly confessional. Our Confessions were often experienced and understood by our fathers and mothers in the faith as life-and-death testimonies on behalf of the gospel.

3.2 In that unique historic setting, such faith testimonies were often expressed in strong polemical language. Such polemic, we have all learned from our bilateral theological conversations among many traditions, often masked and distorted awareness of our common rootedness in the church catholic and its common faith.

3.3 Polemic often leads to caricature and polarization, rarely to careful appreciation of nuances. It is not strange that close cousins within the church catholic have been on occasion the objects of the sharpest polemic and the most unfair caricature. This has often been true for Reformed and Lutheran traditions.

3.4 Yet all of the churches represented in the present dialogue grew out of the same evangelical reform movement of the sixteenth century, and all addressed the same fundamental issues. Our theological reflections often have been expressed in different vocabularies and nuanced somewhat differently from place to place and from time to time in the past four and one-half centuries.

3.5 Our work together in this dialogue persuades us that such a basic consensus now exists among us to justify the conclusion that the condemnations pronounced by the Reformation Confessions are no longer appropriate.[16]

3.6 We affirm that both of our traditions have done their theological reflection from the same foundations and used the same classical vocabulary: Christ alone, faith alone, grace alone, Scripture alone.

3.7 Such affirmation of our unity in Christ is not new among Lutheran and Reformed churches. There have long been examples in America of joint Lutheran-Reformed congregations. We celebrate and call attention to the full fellowship in sacraments and ministries already experienced in Europe for more than ten years under the Leuenberg Agreement.[17]

4. From a common gospel, a common faith, a common theological conviction that Christ intends unity for the church as a faithful reflection of its essential nature, and in obedient response to our Lord's prayer "that they all may be one" (John 17:21);

From a common conviction of the urgency of God's mission confronting identical social, political, and cultural problems which require the united proclamation, witness, and service of Christians;

We therefore request all the members of the Caribbean and North American Area Council (CANAAC) of the World Alliance of Reformed Churches (WARC) and the Lutheran Council in the U.S.A. to receive our report and study it so that there will be the fullest possible use of the document in their own churches. More particularly we call upon the Presbyterian Church (U.S.A.), the Reformed Church in America, the Cumberland Presbyterian Church, the United Church of Christ, the American Lutheran Church, the Association of Evangelical Lutheran Churches, the Lutheran Church in America, and the Lutheran Church—Missouri Synod to take action at their highest levels of authority in order to:

a. Recognize one another as churches in which the gospel is proclaimed and the sacraments administered according to the ordinance of Christ.

b. Recognize as both valid and effective one another's ordained ministries which announce the gospel of Christ and administer the sacraments of faith as their chief responsibility.
c. Recognize one another's celebrations of the Lord's Supper as a means of grace in which Christ grants communion with himself, assures us of the forgiveness of sins, and pledges life eternal.
d. Enter into a process of reception of this report so that it may become a part of the faith and life of each church at the deepest level, moving beyond purely administrative and intellectual action by taking such steps as:
   (1) praying with and for one another, supporting one another's ministry, and where appropriate establishing relationships among presbyteries, classes, conferences, synods, and districts;
   (2) common study at each judicatory level of the Holy Scriptures, the histories and traditions of each church, and current theological and liturgical renewal;
   (3) joint celebrations of the Lord's Supper among congregations, presbyteries, classes, conferences, districts, and synods;
   (4) invitations to the ordained pastors of each tradition to preach in the congregations of the other tradition, and, where local conditions make it necessary or possible, to preside at the Holy Communion of the other tradition;
   (5) designation by each church, in cooperation with the others, of two or three geographical areas where Lutheran and Reformed judicatories serving the same territory might develop extended projects of cooperation, meeting together for joint study of common issues, mission planning, and common worship;
   (6) designation by each regional judicatory of at least one congregation which may be linked in extended projects of cooperation with a congregation of the other tradition, meeting together for joint study of issues, mission planning, and common worship;
   (7) requesting annual reports of such joint ministry, mission, and worship experiences to the national ecumenical offices of the judicatories;
   (8) transmitting a copy of this report and its attached papers to all persons participating in the official response by church bodies to the Lima document on *Baptism, Eucharist and Ministry;*

(9) requesting appointment of a small planning team representing these several ecumenical offices to assemble and evaluate such reports, to report annually to the several churches, and to have responsibility for recommendation of further action appropriate to facilitate this ongoing process of reception;

(10) referring any unresolved theological issues, such as the relationship between faith and ethics, and church and world, to a subsequent dialogue in the context of these new relationships;

(11) informing the World Alliance of Reformed Churches and the Lutheran World Federation of activity and developments in this process of reception.

NOTES

1. See pp. 3–4 for background information.

2. Cf. Appendix 1, Recommendations of LR I, p. 52, below. Cf. Appendix 2, Recommendations of LR II, p. 58, below.

3. Various images and concepts have been used to describe the sacrament in which Christ gives himself anew to the believing community. Among Christians it has been referred to as the Lord's Supper, the Holy Communion, the Sacrament of the Altar, and the Eucharist. Motifs of remembrance, fellowship, thanksgiving, confession and forgiveness, and celebration have been incorporated. Whatever images and concepts are used, the intention and emphasis of the biblical witness and of our traditions have been to assert and affirm God's gift of grace through the body and blood of Christ, "given and shed for you." The several terms, common to our traditions, and to the church catholic, are used interchangeably in the following text: cf. ALC/LCA Statement on Communion Practices, 1978; PC(U.S.A.) *BO* S–3.0500.

4. See description of participating churches, pp. 3–4 above, on the use of Confessions in the UCC.

5. Cf. pp. 9–10, Joint Statement on Justification.

6. FC, Epitome 1:1, *BkC* 464; WC, chap. 1, *BC* 6.001–6.010; BelC, Arts. 3–7; C'67, *BC* 9.27–30; Cumberland Confession of Faith, chaps. 1–4; II HC, *BC* 5.001–2; ScotsC, chap. 19, *BC* 3.19; Constitution, American Lutheran Church, 401; Constitution, Association of Evangelical Lutheran Churches, Article II; Constitution, Lutheran Church in America, Article II, Section 3; PC(U.S.A.) *BO* G–14.0207, 14.0405; Cumberland Constitution chaps. 46, 57. Cf. RCA *Liturgy and Psalms* (ordination service), p. 96.

7. Cf. Appendix 1, *Marburg Revisited*, pp. 42–43; cf. Appendix 3, Leuenberg Agreement, pp. 68–69. Cf. Joint Statement on the Lord's Supper, pp. 14–15, below.

8. Cf. Joint Statement on Ministry, below.

9. Cf. Joint Statement on Ministry, below.

10. CA 1 and 2, *BkC* 27, 29; II HC, chap. 17, *BC* 5.124–41; WC, chap. 25, *BC* 6.125–30; BelC, Arts. 27–28; ScotsC, chap. 16, 18, *BC* 3.16, 3.18; PC(U.S.A.) *BO* G–4.000. For this use of the word "Tradition," see n. 1 of the Joint Statement on Justification, p. 10, below.

11. CA 7, *BkC* 32; BelC, Art. 29; II HC, chap. 17, *BC* 5.134–35; ScotsC, chap. 18, *BC* 3.18.

12. CA 5, *BkC* 31; BelC, chap. 30; ScotsC, chap. 22, *BC* 3.22; WC, chap. 25, *BC* 6.127; II HC, chap. 18, *BC* 5.142–63. According to the Reformed tradition, elders must authorize and be present at the Lord's Supper along with the minister (PC[U.S.A.] *BO* S–3.500).

13. Occasional Services (Companion to the *LBW*), Ordination (Minneapolis: Augsburg Publishing House; Philadelphia: Fortress Press, 1982), p. 193; PC(U.S.A.) *BO* G–11.0203, 14.0401, 15.0202; Cumberland *Constitution*, chap. 60 B; RCA *BCO* I, II 11, 8.

14. *The Ministry of the Church: A Lutheran Understanding* (Division of Theological Studies, Lutheran Council in the U.S.A., 1974), p. 4; II HC, chap. 18, *BC* 5.150–51; PC(U.S.A.) *BO* G–14.0401; Cumberland *Constitution*, chaps. 55–57; RCA *BCO* I, II 10.

15. C'67, *BC* 9.34–40; PC(U.S.A.) *BO* G–2.0200, 3.0401, 4.0303–4, 4.0401.

16. Cf. Appendix 3, Leuenberg Agreement, pp. 66, 69–70, below, esp. paragraphs 5, 20, 23, and 26–28.

17. Cf. Appendix 3, Leuenberg Agreement, pp. 61–73, below.

# MINORITY REPORT

## FROM
## LUTHERAN CHURCH—MISSOURI SYNOD PARTICIPANTS
## OCTOBER 1, 1983

We, The Lutheran Church—Missouri Synod participants, wish to express our gratitude and appreciation for having had the opportunity to participate in Lutheran-Reformed Dialogue III. We commend the participants for their willingness to discuss some of the basic doctrines of the Holy Scripture for the purpose of reaching a better understanding of the faith professed by fellow Christians in other church bodies—with a view toward recognizing their baptism, Lord's Supper, and ministry. We thank God for the amount of agreement which was discovered on the basis of an exchange of views.

A number of substantial issues, however, remain unresolved. Since The Lutheran Church—Missouri Synod establishes altar and pulpit fellowship with other church bodies only after substantial agreement has been reached in all of the doctrines of Scripture, the LCMS participants cannot at this time concur in the opinion that ". . . Lutheran churches should, at the earliest appropriate time and at the highest level, officially recognize the Eucharists (Lord's Suppers) of those churches which affirm the Reformed Confessions and have them as a living part of their present witness and proclamation" [see A Statement of Lutherans to Lutherans Reflecting on This Dialogue, p. 110 of this volume].

We do, however, recommend:

1. that the report of Lutheran-Reformed Dialogue III be forwarded to the president of The Lutheran Church—Missouri Synod with the suggestion that it be shared with the Synod for its information, edification, and mutually agreed-upon action;
2. that The Lutheran Church—Missouri Synod continue to participate in discussions of this kind with a view toward reaching a more complete agreement on the important doctrines of the Scripture; and
3. that we continue fervently to ask God for his guidance and blessing upon our efforts and thus hasten the day when believers everywhere will agree on the truth of God's Holy Word and live together in unity and Christian love.

# JOINT STATEMENT ON JUSTIFICATION

1. Both Lutheran and Reformed churches are evangelical. We are rooted in, live by, proclaim, and confess the gospel of the saving act of God in Jesus Christ. We accept the Tradition[1] of the catholic faith as expressed in the Nicene and Apostles' Creeds.

2. This gospel is the good news that for us and for our salvation God's Son became human in Jesus the Christ, was crucified and raised from the dead. By his life, death, and resurrection he took upon himself God's judgment on human sin and proved God's love for sinners, reconciling the entire world to God.

3. For Christ's sake we sinners have been reconciled to God, not because we earned God's acceptance but by an act of God's sheer mercy. The Holy Spirit calls and enables us to repent of our sin and accept God's gracious offer. Those trusting in this gospel, believing in Christ as Savior and Lord, are justified in God's sight.

4. Both the Lutheran and Reformed traditions confess this gospel in the language of justification by grace through faith alone. This doctrine of justification was the central theological rediscovery of the Reformation; it was proclaimed by Martin Luther and John Calvin and their respective followers.[2]

5. This doctrine of justification continues to be a message of hope and of new life to persons alienated from our gracious God and from one another. Even though Christians who live by faith continue to sin, still in Christ our bondage to sin and death has been broken. By faith we already begin to participate in Christ's victory over evil, the Holy Spirit actively working to redirect our lives.[3]

6. This gospel sets Christians free for good works and responsible service in the whole world. In daily repentance and renewal we praise God and serve others. As grateful servants of God we are enabled to do all those good works that God commands, yet without placing our trust in them. As a community of servants of God we are called and enabled to do works of mercy and to labor for justice and peace among individuals and nations.[4]

## CONCLUSION

7. We agree that there are no substantive matters concerning justification that divide us. We recommend that Lutheran and Reformed churches which subscribe to the classic Confessions of their traditions should at this time officially recognize and declare one another as churches in which the gospel is preached and taught.

### NOTES

1. We distinguish between *Tradition* understood as the common deposit of the faith of the church catholic represented in the canon of Scripture, and *tradition* understood as the ecumenical creeds and traditions of the several faith communities as they have evolved in different periods of history and in different cultures.

2. WC, chap. 11, *BC* 6.060–61:

> Those whom God effectually calleth, he also freely justifieth: not by infusing righteousness into them, but by pardoning their sins, and by accounting and accepting their persons as righteous; not for any thing wrought in them, or done by them, but for Christ's sake alone; not by imputing faith itself, the act of believing, or any other evangelical obedience to them, as their righteousness, but by imputing the obedience and satisfaction of Christ unto them, they receiving and resting on him and his righteousness by faith; which faith they have not of themselves: it is the gift of God. Faith, thus receiving and resting on Christ and his righteousness, is the alone instrument of justification; yet it is not alone in the person justified, but is ever accompanied with all other saving graces, and is no dead faith, but worketh by love.

II HC, chap. 15, *BC* 5.107, 5.109, 5.110:

> Now it is most certain that all of us are by nature sinners and godless, and before God's judgment-seat are convicted of godlessness and are guilty of death, but that, solely by the grace of Christ and not from any merit of ours or consideration for us, we are justified, that is, absolved from sin and death by God the Judge. . . .
>
> But because we receive this justification, not through any works, but through faith in the mercy of God and in Christ, we therefore teach and believe with the apostle that sinful man is justified by faith alone in Christ, not by the law or any works. . . .
>
> Therefore, we do not share in the benefit of justification partly because of the grace of God or Christ, and partly because of ourselves, our love, works or merit, but we attribute it wholly to the grace of God in Christ through faith.

CA 4, *BkC* 30 (German version):

> It is also taught among us that we cannot obtain forgiveness of sin and righteousness before God by our own merits, works, or satisfactions, but that we receive forgiveness of sin and become righteous before God by grace, for Christ's sake, through faith, when we believe that Christ suffered for us and that for his sake our sin is forgiven and righteousness and eternal life are given to us. For God will regard and reckon this faith as righteousness, as Paul says in Romans 3:21–26 and 4:5.

Further evidence of this confessional congruence may be observed: (a) during the Crypto-Calvinist controversy, 1560–74, justification was not an issue (cf. *Book of Concord* [St. Louis: Concordia Publishing House, 1922], pp. 172–92); (b) at Marburg, 1529, Zwingli, Oecolampadius, Bucer, Melanchthon, and Luther agreed on articles on justification (cf. *Book of Concord,* ed. H. E. Jacobs [Philadelphia: Frederick, 1883], II:70–71); (c) the first series of Lutheran-Reformed dialogue in the United States concluded: "We are agreed that the doctrine of justification by faith is fundamental in both traditions. We recognize, however, that for Lutherans this doctrine has played a more formative role in the articulation of theology. This difference is due in part to the historical situations in which Luther and Calvin did their theological work" (cf. Appendix 1, *Marburg Revisited,* p. 44, below); (d) the Leuenberg Agreement, in affirming consensus on justification, had no need to revoke condemnations, as it did on other matters of doctrine (cf. Appendix 3, Leuenberg Agreement, pp. 67–68, below).

In regard to the United Church of Christ's position, it is understood that in 1957 it merged Congregational Christian Churches and the Evangelical and Reformed Church "without break in their respective continuities and traditions" (*Constitution and Bylaws,* p. 3). On the Lutheran side, for example, it thus claims as its own the CA and on the Reformed side the HCat, both confessional statements of the Evangelical and Reformed Church. Thus there is no need to quote again from the CA what already has been noted above. On the Congregational Christian side the Savoy Declaration puts the United Church of Christ in close touch with the WC. The Savoy Declaration was adopted by a Massachusetts Synod in Boston in 1680. Note the close agreement in language with the WC (above, n. 2) on justification:

> Those whom God effectually calleth, he also freely justifieth not by infusing righteousness into them, but by pardoning their sins and by accounting and accepting their person as righteous, not for anything wrought in them, or done by them, but for Christ's sake alone; nor by imputing Faith itself, the act of believing, or any other Evangelical obedience to them, as their righteousness, but by imputing Christ's active obedience unto the whole Law, and passive obedience in his death for their whole and sole righteousness, they receiving and resting on him and his righteousness by Faith; which Faith they have not

> of themselves, it is the gift of God. (Savoy Declaration, chap. 11, in Williston Walker, ed., *The Creeds and Platforms of Congregationalism* [Boston: Pilgrim Press, 1960], pp. 378f.)

3. Both the Lutheran and the Reformed traditions continue to affirm in our confessional statements, our instruction, and our worship that sin is in essence the radical, inveterate, willful self-seeking by which we tend to use our fellow beings and even God for our selfish advantage. Humans are in bondage to sin and thus alienated from God and from one another. Only God through Christ's justifying work can liberate us from this bondage and alienation, reconcile us with God and our fellow humans, and restore the full integrity of all creation.

Both traditions affirm that, although Christians are truly justified in Christ—restored to God's family—our inveterate sinfulness is not eradicated. To describe this situation, Martin Luther occasionally used the paradoxical expression that a Christian is "at one and the same time a righteous person and a sinner" (*simul justus et peccator*). By this he meant that the Christian's life, though truly liberated and righteous in God's sight, is a constant struggle—with the Holy Spirit's help—to eradicate our persisting tendency to fall back into bondage to sin. Both Lutheran and Reformed theologies, however, have traditionally used the term "sanctification" to describe the continuing struggle of the justified Christian, with the Spirit's help, to eliminate his or her sin and manifest a holy life (cf. FC SD 3:40–41, *BkC* 546). Cf. WC VI, *BC* 6.031–36; WC XI, 5, *BC* 6.064; WC XIII, *BC* 6.067–69; WC XV, 3–4, *BC* 6.075–76; II HC VIII–IX, *BC* 5.036–5.051; HCat, Part I, *BC* 4.003–4.011; HCat, Part III, *BC* 4.086–4.129; C'67, *BC* 9:21–26.

Illustrative of this theme in public worship would be the *LBW*, p. 56; *The Worshipbook* of the PC(U.S.A.) and Cumberland Presbyterian Church (jointly published), p. 26; *Book of Common Worship*, PC(U.S.A.), p. 136; *Ordinal and Service Book* of the Church of Scotland, pp. 1–2.

4. CA 6, *BkC* 31–32: "It is also taught among us that such faith should produce good fruits and good works and that we must do all such good works as God has commanded, but we should do them for God's sake and not place our trust in them as if thereby to merit favor before God. . . ." Cf. also CA 20:27,*BkC* 45: "It is also taught among us that good works should and must be done, not that we are to rely on them to earn grace but that we may do God's will and glorify him. It is always faith alone that apprehends grace and forgiveness of sin" and CA 20:35, *BkC* 46: "Consequently this teaching concerning faith is not to be accused of forbidding good works but is rather to be praised for teaching that good works are to be done and for offering help as to how they may be done."

WC, chap. 16, *BC* 6.080–83:

> These good works, done in obedience to God's commandments, are the fruits and evidences of a true and lively faith: and by them believers manifest their thankfulness, strengthen their assurance, edify their brethren, adorn the profession of the gospel, stop the mouths of

the adversaries, and glorify God, whose workmanship they are, created in Jesus Christ thereunto; . . . Their ability to do good works is not at all of themselves, but wholly from the Spirit of Christ. And that they may be enabled thereunto, besides the graces they have already received, there is required an actual influence of the same Holy Spirit to work in them to will and to do of his good pleasure; . . . We cannot, by our best works, merit pardon of sin, or eternal life.

II HC chap. XVI, *BC* 5.118:

Therefore, although we teach with the apostle that a man is justified by grace through faith in Christ and not through any good works, yet we do not think that good works are of little value and condemn them. We know that man was not created or regenerated through faith in order to be idle, but rather that without ceasing he should do those things which are good and useful.

# JOINT STATEMENT ON THE SACRAMENT OF THE LORD'S SUPPER

## GOSPEL

1. We are Christians because of the presence of Jesus Christ in our lives. This good news of Jesus Christ is the gospel. It is from the gospel that we understand the Lord's Supper. The Supper is a unique way in which Christ shares himself with us and in which we share in Christ with one another. Thus the Supper is itself a particular form of the gospel. The same gift is offered in the preached word and in the administered sacrament.[1]

1.1 The gospel is the good news of Jesus Christ, God's Son, who has been given to us because God loves the world and acts to reconcile the world to himself.

1.2 In Christ we are called, corporately and individually, to manifest the presence of our Lord Jesus Christ in our lives, witness, and service. It is this gospel which compels us to engage in God's mission in the world.

1.3 As churches we must see to it that the gospel we proclaim in word and action is indeed the true gospel of the Holy Scriptures and not a distortion or a substitute. This is why both of our communions regard fidelity to the gospel as the fundamental norm for church fellowship.

## GREATNESS OF THE SUPPER

2. Appreciating what we Reformed and Lutheran Christians already hold in common concerning the Lord's Supper, we nevertheless affirm that both of our communions need to keep on growing into an ever-deeper realization of the fullness and richness of the eucharistic mystery.

2.1 Both Lutheran and Reformed churches affirm that Christ himself is the host at his table. Both churches affirm that Christ himself is truly present and received in the Supper. Neither communion professes to explain how this is so.

2.2 The Lord's Supper is inexhaustibly profound and awesome. We concur with the 1982 Lima Faith and Order statement *Baptism, Eucharist and Ministry*, which reminds all Christians that five features belong to the fullness of the Lord's Supper: The Eucharist is (1) thanksgiving to the Father; (2) anamnesis or memorial of Christ; (3) invocation of the Spirit; (4) communion of the faithful; and (5) meal of the kingdom.

2.3 While none of these features is alien to either of our traditions, both Reformed and Lutheran Christians need continually to grow in our understanding and experience of this joyful communion with Christ and with one another.

## THE NEW COMMUNITY

3. By his real presence among us in word and sacrament and by the work of his Holy Spirit, Christ creates and nurtures a new community of faith, his holy church. Holy Communion richly nourishes us in our devotion to a life of faithful discipleship and calls us to grow in our understanding of what God intends the entire human family to become. Fed at Christ's table, we are drawn to care for one another in the fellowship of believers. Fed at Christ's table, we are called to become more sensitive to the needs of our sisters and brothers in the entire human family.

3.1 As we participate in Holy Communion we receive the benefit of the forgiveness of sins, life, and salvation through our trust in God's faithfulness.[2]

3.2 As we participate in Holy Communion with our Lord we experience our oneness in Christ. We become more sensitive to the sufferings of our brothers and sisters in Christ, and we are moved to minister to one another as Christ did.

3.3 As we participate in Holy Communion God commissions us to minister to the entire human family as Christ did. Christ summons us to share our bounty with all those whose physical and spiritual lives are burdened by poverty. He calls us to "... struggle with the oppressed towards that freedom and dignity promised with the coming of the Kingdom" (*BEM*, Ministry, I.4). He challenges us to commit ourselves to the cause of justice and peace for all people.[3]

3.4 As we participate in Holy Communion we are committed afresh to the ecumenical task, the effort to realize Christ's will that all his followers may be one, gathered around one table.

## DOCTRINE

4. We affirm that the Lutheran and Reformed families of churches have a fundamental consensus in the gospel and the sacraments, which not only allows but also demands common participation in the Lord's Supper.

4.1 In the past Christians of the Reformed and Lutheran traditions have been deeply divided by controversy over the understanding of the Lord's Supper although both have strongly affirmed the real presence of Christ in the Sacrament. Today we cherish a high regard for our ancestors in the faith who stalwartly proclaimed the gospel according to their respective convictions. At the same time, through long and careful discussion, responsible commissions of Lutheran and Reformed representatives have concluded that our two communions do fundamentally agree on the gospel and on the sacraments of baptism and the Lord's Supper. We reaffirm these agreements, in particular the conclusions reached in *Marburg Revisited* in America (1966) and the Leuenberg Agreement in Europe (1973). We do not imagine that all differences in eucharistic doctrine between (and within) our two communions have thereby disappeared or become negligible, but we maintain that the remaining differences should be recognized as acceptable diversities within one Christian faith.[4]

4.2 The Christian doctrine of the Lord's Supper needs to present the clearest and fullest possible witness to the profound meaning of the Supper. We maintain that traditional Lutheran and Reformed doctrinal concerns are still valuable to help the wider Christian community appreciate the full significance of our Lord's Supper. We acknowledge meanwhile that our doctrinal formulations themselves cannot altogether grasp the fullness either of the mystery of Christ's gift of himself in the Supper or of our experience of communion with him.

## PRACTICE

5. Mutual recognition of the Lord's Supper by our two communions also involves reconciliation in regard to our appreciation of each other's eucharistic practice.

5.1 As churches of the Reformation we share many important features in our respective practices of Holy Communion. Over the centuries of our separation, however, there have developed characteristic differences in practice, and these still tend to make us uncomfortable at each other's celebration of the Supper. These differences can be discerned in several areas, for example, in liturgical style and liturgical details, in our verbal interpretations of our practices, in the emotional patterns involved in our experience of the Lord's Supper, and in the implications we find in the Supper for the life and mission of the church and of its individual members.[5]

5.2 We affirm our conviction, however, that these differences should be recognized as acceptable diversities within one Christian faith. Both of our communions, we maintain, need to grow in appreciation of our diverse eucharistic traditions, finding mutual enrichment in them. At the same time both need to grow toward a further deepening of our common experience and expression of the mystery of our Lord's Supper.

## MINISTRY

6. Reconciliation at the Lord's Table also involves mutual recognition of our public ministries, since each church is responsible for authorizing and publicly regulating the celebration of the Lord's Supper.[6]

## CONCLUSION

7. We agree that there are no substantive matters concerning the Lord's Supper which should divide us. We urge Lutheran and Reformed churches to affirm and encourage the practice of eucharistic fellowship with one another.

### NOTES

1. On the variety of names applied to this sacrament, see n. 3 of An Invitation to Action.

2. "... the forgiveness of sins, life, and salvation are given to us in the sacrament, for where there is forgiveness of sins, there are also life and salvation" (SC 6:6, *BkC* 352). Both Martin Luther and John Calvin stressed the benefits of the sacrament. Luther described the sacrament as "rich in grace . . . full of benefit and salvation, as well as innumerable and unspeakable blessings" ("Admonition Concerning the Sacrament," *Luther's Works*, Vol. 38 [Philadelphia: Fortress Press, 1971], p. 105). Among such benefits and blessings he included being "present to the praise of glory of God" (p. 109), having "faith and love stimulated, renewed and strengthened" (pp. 125f.), "the heart is refreshed anew in its love of the neighbor and is made strong and equipped to do all good works and to resist sin and all temptations" (p. 126). Calvin speaks of the Lord's Supper as a "spiritual banquet, wherein Christ attests himself to be

the life-giving bread, upon which our souls feed unto true and blessed immortality" (*Institutes of the Christian Religion* IV, xvii, 1, ed. J. T. McNeill [Philadelphia: Westminster Press, 1960], p. 1360). "Godly souls can gather great assurance and delight from this Sacrament; in it they have a witness of our growth into one body with Christ such that whatever is his may be called ours." We are assured of participation in eternal life, the Kingdom of Heaven, and forgiveness of sin (*Inst.* IV, xvii, 2, pp. 1361–62). Participation in the one body of Christ inspires "purity and holiness of life" and "love, peace, and concord"; so the Sacrament is a "bond of love" arousing mutual love in the community (*Inst.* IV, xvii, 38, pp. 1414–15). For Calvin's view of the real presence of Christ in the Eucharist, see *Inst.* IV, xvii, 1–33 esp. 7, 10, 14, 18, 19, 31, 32.

The Savoy Declaration (Williston Walker, ed., *The Creeds and Platforms of Congregationalism* [Boston: Pilgrim Press, 1960], p. 400) corresponds with the WC also on the Lord's Supper (see n. 2, Joint Statement on Justification). The CA in the UCC of course offers the same tradition as noted here.

3. "God's reconciliation in Jesus Christ is the ground of the peace, justice, and freedom among nations which all powers of government are called to serve and defend. The church, in its own life, is called to practice the forgiveness of enemies and to commend to the nations as practical politics the search for cooperation and peace" (C'67, *BC* 9.45). "The reconciliation of man [*sic*] through Jesus Christ makes it plain that enslaving poverty in a world of abundance is an intolerable violation of God's good creation. Because Jesus identified himself with the needy and exploited, the cause of the world's poor is the cause of his disciples" (C'67, *BC* 9.46). "The Holy Communion is a service celebrating reconciliation. It is a Means of Grace by which the common life of God's new community is fostered and sustained and this new people is propelled into the world to engage in the mission which they have been given" (A Statement on Communion Practices, I.6, Appendix 4, p. 78).

One of the summary statements on ethics formulated and adopted by both Lutheran and Reformed theologians states: "This world is the arena for Christian ethical service. The impersonal structures of power in modern society are morally ambiguous. While they tend to pervert the humanity of men [*sic*] and the proper use of things, they also offer untold possibilities for good. This situation compels us to search for new ways of loving our neighbors. Recent technological and sociological developments intensify the urgency for translating personal love into social justice" ("Christian Service in the Modern World," *Marburg Revisited*, ed. Paul C. Empie and James I. McCord [Minneapolis: Augsburg Publishing House, 1966], p. 177; below p. 45).

4. Insistence on the importance of affirming real presence and sacramental union is prominent in both Lutheran and Reformed traditions. II HC asserts that "by the work of Christ through the Holy Spirit they (the faithful) inwardly receive the flesh and blood of the Lord, and are thereby nourished unto life eternal. For the flesh and blood of Christ is the true food and drink unto life eternal; and Christ himself, since he was given for us and is our Savior, is the principal thing in the Supper . . ." (*BC* 5.196). Similarly the ScotsC announces

that "we utterly condemn the vanity of those who affirm the sacraments to be nothing else than naked and bare signs," and insists that ". . . in the Supper rightly used, Christ Jesus is so joined with us that he becomes the very nourishment and food of our souls" (*BC* 3.21). CA 10 affirms "that the true body and blood of Christ are really present in the Supper of our Lord under the form of bread and wine and are there distributed and received" (*BkC* 34), which the Ap 10 expands: ". . . that in the Lord's Supper the body and blood of Christ are truly and substantially present and are truly offered with those things that are seen, the bread and the wine. We are talking about the presence of the living Christ, knowing that 'death no longer has dominion over him'" (*BkC* 179–80).

The controversy has focused on the mode of Christ's presence in the sacrament. The signers of FC SD 7 rejected "the denial of an oral eating of the body and blood of Christ in the Supper, and the contrary teaching that in the Supper the body of Christ is partaken only spiritually through faith and that in the Supper our mouth receives only bread and wine" (*BkC* 589). The WC holds that "worthy receivers, outwardly partaking of the visible elements in this sacrament, do then also inwardly by faith, really and indeed, yet not carnally and corporally, but spiritually, receive and feed upon Christ crucified, and all benefits of his death: the body and blood of Christ being then not corporally or carnally in, with, or under the bread and wine; yet, as really, but spiritually, present to the faith of believers in that ordinance as the elements themselves are to their outward senses" (*BC* 6.152).

Both traditions were trying to protect and preserve the dynamic of authentic sacramental union between Christ, the believer, and the other faithful over against the opposing extremes of mere symbolic recollection and the magic of transubstantiation. Each tradition suspected that the other veered too far toward one of the unacceptable extremes.

In recent times scholars have approached the problems from fresh and helpful directions. For example, the Lutheran scholar Regin Prenter gives the expected emphasis on divine promise: "In every sacrament there is a divine *promissio* expressed in the Word which accompanies the sacrament. This *promissio* is the decisive factor. It is what makes the sacrament a sacrament." Then Prenter continues: "By virtue of understanding the word of the sacrament as *promissio* faith enters into the concept of the sacrament in the sense that it thus forms the real connection between the Word and the external element. For the external element is the confirmation of the promise. But only faith in the promise can receive the confirmation" (*Spiritus Creator*, trans. J. M. Jensen [Philadelphia: Muhlenberg Press, 1953], pp. 138f.).

Oscar Cullmann writes: "[Christ's] presence is understood to be as real as possible. He comes to participate in the meal. . . . In the early Church, the Lord's Supper involved the presence of Christ in its threefold relation with Easter, with the cult and with Parousia. Alternatively expressed, this presence is at one and the same time that of Christ risen, of Christ living, and of Christ who is to come" ("The Meaning of the Lord's Supper," *Essays on the Lord's Supper*, trans. J. G. Davies [Atlanta: John Knox Press, 1958], p. 15). Reformed Christians feel at home with such formulations. A contemporary Reformed declaration of faith affirms:

> The Word has not only been read and preached,
> But also seen, tasted, and touched.
>
> We believe Christ is present through the Spirit of the Lord's Supper.
> He makes himself known to us as the one who stood in our place and conquered our death for us.
> He offers us his broken body and shed blood.
> We offer ourselves to him in return.
>
> A Declaration of Faith, chap. 6, lines 93–94, 112–18, PCUS, Atlanta, 1974

David Willis focuses on Christ's real presence in "The Eucharist in the Reformed Tradition," prepared for the Russian Orthodox/Reformed Consultations (Leningrad, 1976).

Wilhelm Niesel describes a meeting of the Confessional Synod of the Evangelical Church of the Old Prussian Union which met in Halle in 1937 and affirmed "Our Lord and Saviour Jesus Christ . . . is Himself the gracious gift in the Supper He instituted in His church. . . . The differences still existing between us in the doctrine of the Holy Supper concern the mode and form in which the Lord gives Himself in the supper. They do not touch the fact that the gift in the Supper is the Lord Himself." Niesel further reports on the theses published in 1957 after eight years of study by a commission of theologians from the Lutheran, Reformed, and Union churches which states: "The words spoken by our Lord Jesus Christ, in offering to us the bread and the cup, tell us what He Himself gives in this supper to all who came to it. He, the crucified and risen Lord, permits Himself in His body delivered to death for all and in His blood shed for all, to be taken by us through His promised Word with the bread and the wine, and thereby associates us, by the power of the Holy Spirit, with the victory of His Kingdom so that, by faith in His promise, we have forgiveness of sins, life and salvation" (*The Gospel and the Churches,* trans. D. Lewis [Philadelphia: Westminster Press, 1962], pp. 282–83).

These affirmations led Niesel to conclude that "theologians of the different Reformation Churches can today bear common testimony on the basis of Scripture about the meaning of the Lord's Supper," and "Membership of one or the other of the Reformation Churches therefore constitutes no ground for exclusion from celebrations of the Lord's Supper" (ibid.). Subsequent Lutheran-Reformed affirmations such as *Marburg Revisited* (1966), the Leuenberg Agreement (1973), and the Lima statement on *Baptism, Eucharist and Ministry* (1982) encourage us to embrace similar conclusions.

The difficulty of translating theological concepts and religious insights from one language to another has been expressed throughout the history of the church as it has grown and expanded among all peoples and cultures. Biblical translators such as Luther and Calvin and their successors struggled with the problems of finding appropriate words and phrases in Latin, German, and

French, for example, that would accurately represent the Hebrew and Greek originals.

The framers of the *BkC*, as well as authors of other Reformation confessional statements, also faced this dilemma. As the preface to the *BkC* affirms: "we repeat once again that we are not minded to manufacture anything new by this work of agreement or to depart in any way at all, either in content or in formulation, from the divine truth that our pious forebears and we have acknowledged and confessed in the past" (p. 13). Nevertheless, the preface acknowledges honest differences of opinion and interpretation which required "a general convention . . . to discuss in a thorough and friendly way" such differences with the intent that such "offensive differences might be settled and brought to a conclusion (*consensus*) without violation of divine truth . . ." (pp. 4–6).

There is a recognition that in technical theological questions such as the relation of the idea of omnipresence to the Lord's Supper, it is advisable "to stay with the plain words of Christ." "This," they say, "is the surest and most edifying way as far as the common layman is concerned, for he cannot comprehend this discussion" (*BkC*, p. 10).

Furthermore, changes in scientific and philosophical outlooks from one period of history to another also present problems of "translating" traditional doctrines. The truth of God's revelation in Jesus Christ is changeless, but the human language which gives it doctrinal expression undergoes constant modification. We realize that while the sixteenth-century formulations of doctrines such as the real presence represent faithful articulations of the biblical message, they also were conditioned by the worldview of the period. Our world is strikingly different from that of Luther and Calvin and their contemporaries, and the words and phrases now used to interpret the mysteries of our faith may take on unintended meaning or lose their original import. The task of "translating" traditional doctrines into a language which mirrors the worldview of our times presents both a challenge and new possibilities. The challenge of setting ancient formulations in the context of twentieth-century thought is formidable. But it is possible that this process will shed new light on ancient texts. We believe that as this "translating" continues, Lutheran and Reformed Christians will increasingly discover that what divided their forebears in regard to the Lord's Supper need not be divisive; to the contrary, classical Reformed and Lutheran concerns over the real presence may come to be seen as complementary and enriching for the lives of both traditions.

This does not settle the matter, of course, but it suggests that the deepest articles of faith, in whatever language, are ultimately, as the theologians of the *Book of Concord* admit, in the realms of "inscrutable mystery."

In A Statement on Communion Practices both The American Lutheran Church and the Lutheran Church in America exhorted Lutherans to ". . . uphold the reality of Christ's presence in the Sacrament, his body and blood being given 'in, with and under' the bread and the wine, in order to affirm by these means his saving work for us." To this point the paper comments, "It is the responsibility of our churches to teach clearly this Lutheran doctrine of the Lord's Supper and to witness to it in dealing with other churches. Fulfilling the obligation to the truth in this way makes it possible to express the unity of the Church at the Lord's table with those who affirm the Real Presence of Christ in the Sacrament *but who use formulations to describe it other than those used in the Lutheran Confessions*" (p. 4; or pp. 76–77 of this volume; emphasis added).

5. Considerable diversity in the practices of celebrating the Lord's Supper exists among congregations of both the Lutheran and the Reformed traditions. Partly this is a consequence of denominational divergence; partly it reflects the impact of regional custom. In recent years the influence of liturgical renewal (including recovery of the liturgical heritage of the tradition) and of liturgical experimentation has increased the rate of diversity.

For example, some Reformed and UCC congregations stand or even are seated around the communion table for the distribution of the elements. The more usual method in the United States, however, is for communicants to serve each other from trays passed down the pews. Even this more usual custom is ambiguous to worshippers. Some regard it as simply an arrangement of convenience. For others it is a moving visual enactment of the priesthood of all believers.

Lutheran practice at the Supper also varies: communicants may come to the altar and stand or kneel; administration may be by table or continuous; stations in several parts of the building may be used; communicants may stand in a circle and administer the bread and wine to each other; use of the chalice is preferred, but many congregations use individual glasses; wine is the norm, but some congregations use grape juice; either leavened or unleavened bread is used; intinction is occasionally used; it is normal to include lay persons in the distribution of the elements, but in many congregations only the pastor distributes. Lutherans have experienced a rich growth in practice over the past twenty-five years.

There are central features that are characteristic of Reformed observance as testified by the constitutional documents of the churches:

Regular or frequent celebrations of the sacrament: "at least once every three months" (RCA *BCO* 1.I.2.6.c); "frequently but at least quarterly" (PCUS *BCO* 211–12); "as frequently as each Lord's Day, and at least as often as quarterly" (PC[U.S.A.], *BO* S–3.05005); cf. also *Confession of Faith* of the Cumberland Presbyterian Church, p. 160, 18.

The sacrament is held in high regard—"an essential part of the public ministry of the church," PC(U.S.A.) *BO* S–3.0100; cf. also the WC chap. 27, 1, *BC* 6.134; UPCUSA, *BO* 21.

The unworthy are to be warned: PC(U.S.A.) *BO* S–3.0500d; cf. RCA "Orders for Public Worship," *Liturgy and Psalms*, p. 77; "The minister shall also warn the unprepared, the self-sufficient, the unrepentant, not to approach the holy table" (PCUS *BCO* 211–17).

The elements used are bread and wine, although many congregations substitute unfermented grape juice: PC(U.S.A.) *BO* S–3.0500e; *Confession of*

*Faith* of the Cumberland Presbyterian Church, pp. 161f., n. 20; PCUS *BCO*, 211–18.

The distribution of the elements is preceded by an *epiklesis* and the repetition of the scriptural words of institution—"the minister . . . shall ask that the Holy Spirit sanctify the Sacrament to the people's benefit" PC(U.S.A.) *BO* S-3.0500f, g; PCUS *BCO* 211–17, 18. "The invocation of the Holy Spirit signifies and seeks to ensure that what takes place in the sacrament is not accomplished by human endeavor, but is done by the grace of God" UPCUSA *BO*, 21.03. "Great God, give your Holy Spirit in the breaking of bread, so that we may be drawn together, joined to Christ the Lord, receive new life, and remain his glad and faithful people until we feast with him in glory" (*The Worshipbook* [Philadelphia: Westminster Press, 1970], p. 36).

The norm of Lutheran practice for the LCA and the ALC is contained in A Statement on Communion Practices, adopted in 1978 (Appendix 4). There is no comparable document for the AELC.

The Supper is described as a sacrament, "God's gift of Christ's presence and love to us"; "a service celebrating reconciliation"; "a means of grace by which the common life of God's new community is fostered and sustained," and "this new people is propelled into the world to engage in the mission. . . ."

Admission is open to the baptized who in the judgment of the church are ready to participate. Criteria for readiness include: "simple trust that the Crucified and Risen Lord is here truly present"; "basic understanding and appreciation of the gifts . . ."; "acceptance of one's place as a communicant in the fellowship of believers"; "self-examination . . . appropriate to the level of maturity and recognition of the need for forgiveness."

Corporate confession and absolution are of "great value" and a "normal preparation." Opportunity for private confession is recommended.

Participation as a visitor in non-Lutheran settings is "proper" and "a matter of personal judgment." Five criteria are offered. Lutheran clergy may be involved as presiding or assisting ministers in other churches if a "reciprocal relationship between the congregation and clergy involved should prevail."

Celebration of Holy Communion is recommended on every Sunday and on other festivals, and on weekdays for those "whose schedules make Sunday communion difficult."

Lutherans use the elements of bread and wine. The elements, according to the *LBW*, may be set aside by the words of institution alone, a prayer and words of institution, or a eucharistic prayer.

6. This brief section intends to direct attention to the companion statement by the Lutheran-Reformed dialogue entitled Joint Statement on Ministry, pp. 24–31.

# JOINT STATEMENT ON MINISTRY

## OUR COMMON HERITAGE

1. The traditions we represent are *rooted in a common understanding* of the gospel which developed at the time of the Reformation.

1.1 What we hold in common is fundamental to both Reformation traditions. For both Lutheran and Reformed believers the cornerstone of faith is expressed in the Reformation's Confession of *salvation through Christ alone*. Standing alongside of it are those other great affirmations of the sixteenth century, namely, faith alone (*sola fide*), grace alone (*sola gratia*), and Scripture alone (*sola scriptura*). That which is the ground for salvation is also the foundation for ministry. Ministry in our heritage derives from and points to the Christ who alone is sufficient to save. Centered in the proclamation of the word and administration of the sacraments, it is built on the affirmation that the benefits of Christ are known only through faith, grace, and Scripture. Ministry in the Reformation perspective always draws attention away from itself to the Lord it serves and at the same time to those the Lord loves and seeks to redeem.[1]

## THE SERVANT MINISTRY OF JESUS AND OUR MINISTRY

2. There is but *one ministry, that of Jesus Christ*. In all its aspects this was a *servant* ministry. All ministry in the church derives from the ministry of its Lord and is also characterized by service.

2.1 The relationship of the ministry of Jesus to ours has been well expressed by the dictum that speaks of the ministry of the church participating in the great ministry of its Lord. As he is the truth which frees men and women, so the church through its ministry by the power of the Holy Spirit proclaims this liberating truth in word and deed. As he is the sacrificial lamb offered for forgiveness and reconciliation, so the church announces this free gift of love and acts as an agent of healing and reconciliation. As he is the hidden ruler of the world, the church reveals to humankind its true Lord, calls all people to a life of worship, and participates in the divine acts of justice and mercy which witness to God's sovereign power and majesty.[2]

2.2 The biblical term "servant" best captures the understanding of ministry we hold in common. To speak of a servant ministry is redundant, for the word "ministry" *means* service in its own right. At the same time, it is necessary to tolerate this redundancy and join the words, for the unhappy truth is that today the word "ministry" does not always connote service.[3]

2.3 This is unfortunate, for the only way to participate in the ministry of the one who came not to be served but to serve is through engaging in a servant ministry. The writers of the New Testament saw Jesus as the servant par excellence. His life is presented as one of perfect obedience to God and consequently one of humble service to humanity. The Lord taught his disciples that greatness in his kingdom means becoming a servant of all (Mark 10:44). "Jesus made his own the nature, condition and cause of the whole human race, giving himself as a sacrifice for all. Jesus' life of service, his death and resurrection, are the foundation of a new community which is built up continually by the good news of the Gospel and the gifts of the sacraments" (*BEM*, Ministry, I.1).[4]

## MINISTRY AND THE KINGDOM OF GOD

3. Christian ministry is oriented to the kindgom of God. In the power of the Spirit it serves Christ both in the church and the world by seeking to manifest signs of the salvation to come.

3.1 The Holy Spirit calls, gathers, enlightens, and sanctifies a people to serve the lordship of Christ (the *regnum Christi*), which will come in its fullness only when Christ returns at the end of history. The kingdom of God is truly present here and now through signs created when the Spirit of Christ engages the people of God in the servant tasks of the Lord. By these signs the world is given testimony of the church's belief in the triumph of God's love and witness to its faith in the advent of a new age when all things shall be made new. These signs are established when the church, in obedience to its Lord and in the power of the Spirit, becomes an agent of justice, mercy, peace, healing, and reconciliation in this world. But the signs of the new age are also present when within the church lives are reborn, healed, reconciled, and sanctified; when in Christian community persons are knit in love, united in service, and joined in proclaiming the gospel; when God's people gather to acknowledge their dependence on grace, openly confess Christ, and publicly glorify the triune God.[5]

## THE MINISTRY OF THE ENTIRE PEOPLE OF GOD

4. The entire baptized people of God, the body of Christ, is called to participate in Christ's servant ministry. The foundation for this vision of ministry is to be found in the Reformation doctrines of the universal priesthood of all believers and Christian vocation.

4.1 The servant ministry is the people of God engaged in God's mission (the *missio Dei*), the service of the kingdom. The call to this service is not limited to those who hold office in the church but is extended to all who are baptized. As stated above, the cornerstone for the Reformation doctrine of ministry is salvation through Christ alone. Union with Christ in baptism carries with it the call, power, authority, and promise of gifts requisite for the participation in his servant ministry. For example, immediately following the imposition of water, according to the baptismal liturgy of the Reformed Church in America, the officiant declares: "In the name of the Lord Jesus Christ, the only King and Head of his Church, I declare that this child is now received into the visible membership of the Holy Catholic Church, and is engaged to confess the faith of Christ crucified, and to be his faithful servant unto his/her life's end." Here all distinctions are rejected. Male and female, young and old, impaired and unimpaired, educated and uneducated, rich and poor, people of every color, nation, and tongue—all who are baptized and confess Christ are also called to be part of the servant ministry. This ministry is the ministry of the entire people of God.[6]

4.2 The Reformation spoke of this doctrine as the universal priesthood of all believers. Formulated by Martin Luther, the notion of the universal priesthood was recognized as profoundly biblical by Reformation theologians, and it consequently became critical for the development of ministry in both traditions. All Christians are called and empowered by the Holy Spirit to be priests to their neighbors. This means that worship, intercession, service, and witness are not reserved for the clergy but are the responsibility of all believers. The pastoral office is instituted to strengthen and support the community of believers.[7]

4.3 The scope of the servant ministry of the entire people of God becomes apparent, however, only when the Reformation doctrine of vocation is also taken into consideration. Both the Lutheran and Reformed theologians of the Reformation rejected the medieval distinction between higher and lower occupations. God calls men and women to employment not only in the church but in the secular world as well.

Any task that contributes to the preservation of the created order, the well-being of humankind, and the administration of justice is pleasing to God. Christians are called to engage their vocations honestly, justly, and as a service to God and neighbor. Then even the most humble and mundane tasks are rightly viewed as service to God.[8]

4.4 The implications for the mission of God of these two Reformation doctrines are far-reaching. The ministry of every baptized Christian is exercised through vocation in both church and world. Since the lordship of Christ is the priestly rule of the one who offers himself as the sacrificial lamb, the universal priesthood represents the self-offering of the people of God in the service of the kingdom. The Spirit bestows diverse gifts on God's people not only to build up the church but also to establish signs of the kingdom in the world. The church aids in the identification and development of these gifts both to strengthen the bond of love within its own fellowship and its witness in word and deed in the world. The church also learns from those who work in the secular order about pressing human needs and strategies to address them. Persons at work in the world are equipped by the church for their vocation in the larger society, but they in turn help to shape the church's understanding of its mission.

## THE PASTORAL OFFICE

5. In the context of the ministry of the whole people of God, the pastoral office is accorded special servant responsibility.

5.1 To affirm the servant ministry of the entire people of God and the Reformation doctrines of the universal priesthood and Christian vocation does not mean that all are called to the same places and tasks in the church. Lutheran and Reformed Christians alike can agree with the Lima document, *Baptism, Eucharist and Ministry*, when it states: "In order to fulfil its mission, the Church needs persons who are publicly and continually responsible for pointing to its fundamental dependence on Jesus Christ, and thereby provide, within a multiplicity of gifts, a focus of its unity" (*Ministry*, IIA. 8). For both the Lutheran and Reformed traditions the ordained office of pastor has borne much of the responsibility for this task.[9]

5.2 To set the pastoral office (minister of the word) in the context of the servant ministry of the baptized people of God does not deny its special character. Our Confessions speak of this as a divinely appointed office. While we do not contend that one particular form of this office has divine sanction to the exclusion of others, we do hold the office itself to be an expression of the will of God for the church. Indeed, the

Reformation understanding of word and sacraments as means of grace is very closely tied to the Lutheran and Reformed doctrines of the pastoral office. God deigns to use ordained ministers as instruments to mediate grace through the preaching of the word and the administration of the sacraments.[10]

## THE SERVANT MINISTRY OF THE PASTORAL OFFICE

6. The pastoral office is exalted by the service that characterizes it; in its every aspect this office is expressive of the servant ministry.

6.1 The pastoral ministry has been termed a high calling, and rightly so, but only because it serves a Lord exalted through humiliation and raised gloriously from the shame and ignominy of crucifixion. The paradoxical character of Jesus' ministry shapes the pastoral office. Its power is manifested not in strength but weakness; its authority does not reside in itself but is derived from its Lord. In a world that extols autonomy, the pastoral ministry is openly dependent; in an age that insists on pursuing its self-centered interests, this office finds its meaning in serving others. The exalted lowliness of the pastoral ministry is not only its glory but its freedom as well. Luther's dictum that the truly free person is one in servitude to Christ has special meaning in this connection.[11]

6.2 As effected in the universal priesthood, every aspect of the pastoral office should be marked by its participation in the servant ministry of Christ. Standing under the authority of the word, this ministry is exercised in concert with the congregation in witness to the world. The shape of the pastoral office as our churches have experienced it since the Reformation has many commonalities. The styles of exercise of pastoral ministry have always been adapted to changing historical and cultural circumstances. This process of adaptation of style and form will continue though the fundamental purpose remains. The pastoral office with special responsibility for upbuilding the congregation is a servant ministry enabling the baptized to become a servant community in the world. Pastors use their gifts and training to assist all the members of the community to grow in faith, to minister to one another in love, to discern their special gifts, and to develop their knowledge and skills for ministry. In this way the community can become one prepared to serve the world. But it is also for the sake of the world, so that the people of God may truly serve the Lord who claims sovereignty over all of creation, working for the transformation of the whole created order according to the will of God.

## MISSION AND ORDER

7. Structure serves the mission of the church.

7.1 One of the points at which the Lutheran and Reformed traditions have differed is church order. We are convinced that these differences are not church-dividing. Within each tradition, moreover, there is considerable diversity in order. Both our traditions have insisted that church order is not an end in itself and that no one order is biblically mandated to the exclusion of all others. Were one to speak of a biblical imperative on this matter, then it would be that structure must serve the mission of the church.[12]

## MINISTRY AND ORDINATIONS

8. Lutheran and Reformed Christians are in basic agreement concerning the nature and function of the ordained pastoral office. Churches of the Reformed tradition have also ordained elders and deacons.

8.1 The ordering of the serving community can be discussed under two headings: ordination and oversight. In regard to ordination to the pastoral office there are broad areas of agreement uniting Lutheran and Reformed Christians. Both traditions assert that men and women alike are eligible for this office but also must be called, examined for fitness, educated theologically, and approved by the appropriate judicatory. Both understand ordination to be the induction to an office in the church which carries with it certain necessary functions. For both Lutherans and Reformed ordination requires prayer and the laying on of hands and is viewed as a rite by which the candidate enters an office in the church universal. Reordination is rare in both traditions. The authority of the office is the word of God, and this is also its content. Both traditions have insisted that this apostolic office, which finds its center in the preaching of the word and the administration of the sacraments, be anchored in the Confessions and creeds of the church.

8.2 At the same time the Reformed tradition has set the pastoral office in a broader ministerium which includes ordained elders who share the government and oversight of the church and ordained deacons who are given responsibility for ministries of compassion and justice directed to those in need both in the church and in the world. While the Lutheran tradition has restricted ordination to the ministry of word and sacraments, it commissions or sets apart lay persons for particular ministries of leadership and governance in the church and compassion and justice in both church and world.[13]

## MINISTRY AND OVERSIGHT

9. Both the Lutheran and Reformed traditions agree that oversight is necessary for the well-being of the church and the prosperity of its ministry.

9.1 Our two traditions also agree in the understanding that appropriate structures are requisite for proper oversight to be given to the church of Jesus Christ. The nomenclature, organization, and mode of operation may differ, but the objective of strengthening the church and giving guidance to its servant ministry is identical.[14]

9.2 Both the Lutheran and Reformed traditions have believed it important for congregations to be related to one another. Structures have been developed in both traditions by which this has been accomplished and the oversight of congregations corporately exercised. In neither case is governance limited to pastors. In the Reformed tradition elders share with ministers the task of exercising oversight; in the Lutheran tradition lay leaders elected by the congregations share with those holding the pastoral office the responsibility of overseeing congregations on the synodical or district levels.

9.3 The title "bishop" is rarely used in Reformed churches to refer to one who exercises oversight, while it has become common in the Lutheran tradition. It should be noted that Lutheran polity, like Reformed, is constitutional, establishing procedures for electing and removing bishops, defining their responsibilities and authority, and expressing the manner in which those holding this office shall be held accountable. All the functions of the Lutheran bishop in North America are carried out in relationship to a synod, district, or church body.

Reformed Christians have on occasion spoken of their presbyteries (or associations or classes) as corporate bishops. Presbyteries or classes, comprised of ministers of the word and elders who share equally in the work, exercise oversight over a limited number of congregations clustered in a specified region. This oversight includes the supervising and ordaining of candidates for ministry, approving the call of a congregation to a minister, examining its provisions to see that the pastor is properly cared for, determining that a congregation is being properly served by its pastor, disciplining ministers, and granting the right of a congregation to acquire and dispose of property.

The bishop, together with the synod or district in the Lutheran tradition and the presbytery in the Reformed, bears responsibility for the general well-being of the congregations to which he or she gives oversight and assures that the activities of the churches are undertaken in an orderly fashion.[15]

9.4 Both our ecclesial families claim to stand in the historical and apostolic tradition by which the good news of the gospel is given witness generation after generation. Both traditions assert that proper oversight is requisite to ensure that the word is truly preached and sacraments rightly administered.

## CONCLUSION

10. We agree that there are no substantive matters concerning ministry which should divide us. We urge Lutheran and Reformed churches to affirm and recognize the validity of one another's ministries.[16]

## NOTES

1. The Lutheran and Reformed Confessions of the sixteenth and seventeenth centuries abound in references to the *solus Christus*. For specific references see the frequently quoted first question of the HCat, *BC* 4.001, as well as Q. 29 and Q. 30 (4.029 and 4.030); the II HC which speaks of God being invoked only through Christ (*BC* 5.024) and Jesus as the only means of salvation (*BC* 5.077); and further the BelC, articles 20–22, and the WC, chap. 8, *BC* 6.043–6.050. For references in the Lutheran symbols see the CA 4 on justification, *BkC* 30 and also CA 21, *BkC* 47, 2–4; Ap 4, *BkC* 107–68, where in an extended discussion of the Reformation doctrine of justification the *solus Christus* is constantly asserted; and further the SA II, I, *BkC* 292.

For the Lutheran confessional affirmation of the *sola fide*, see CA 4, *BkC* 30; Ap 4, *BkC* 107–68; SA II, I, *BkC* 292. For the same doctrine in the Reformed standards see HCat Q. 20 and Q. 21, *BC* 4.020 and 4.021, and Q. 53 and Q. 61, *BC* 4.053 and 4.061; II HC, chaps. 15 and 16, *BC* 5.106–5.123; BelC, article 22; WC, chap. 11, *BC* 6.060 and 6.061. The doctrine of the *sola gratia* appears in many of the citations already given but see also Luther's LC on the third article of the Apostles' Creed for a forceful exposition of the relation of salvation to word and Spirit (*BkC* 415–16, ##38–42). For references in the Reformed confessional statements in addition to the above, see HCat Q. 60, *BC* 4.060, and II HC, chaps. 10 and 14, *BC* 5.052 and 5.094. Since it is well known that the *sola scriptura* is the foundational principle both for the theology of the Reformation and for both Lutheran and Reformed confessional statements, no specific citations will be offered.

In regard to the UCC position, see the introduction to An Invitation to Action and n. 2 of the Joint Statement of Justification. The *sola scriptura* principle is quite clear also from the Congregational side: "The partes [*sic*] of Church-Government are all of them exactly described in the word of God. . . . So that it is not left in the power of men, officers, Churches, or any state in the world to add, or diminish, or alter anything in the least measure therein" (Cambridge Platform, p. 203).

Cf. CA 7, *BkC* 32: "Also they teach that one holy church is to continue forever. The church is the congregation of saints, in which the Gospel is rightly taught and the Sacraments rightly administered. And to the true unity of the church, it is enough to agree concerning the doctrine of the Gospel and the administration of the Sacraments. Nor is it necessary that human traditions, that is, rites, or ceremonies, instituted by men, should be everywhere alike. As Paul says: 'One faith, one baptism, one God and Father of all.'" Cf. II HC, chap. 17, *BC* 5.141, a parallel Reformed statement.

2. Concerning the point that the ministry of the church participates in the ministry of the ascended Christ, see Ap 7 and 8, ##28 and 47, *BkC* 173 and 177, where the pastoral office is described as standing in Christ's stead. This is also implicit in CA 5 and 8, cf. 28, #22, *BkC* 31, 33, 84. See also the LCA Constitution, Article II (Confession of Faith), section 2: "In [Jesus Christ], the Word Incarnate, God imparts Himself to His people"; Article IV (Nature of the Church), section 1: "All power in the Church belongs to our Lord Jesus Christ, its head. All actions of this church [i.e., the LCA] are to be carried out under His rule and authority" (cf. ALC Constitution and Bylaws, 4.11). For the Reformed Confessions on this: II HC chaps. 14 and 18, *BC* 5.096–5.100 and 5.142–168, passim; BelC, articles 34 and 35 where the ministry of Christ is described as being effected by human agents; WC, chap. 25, *BC* 6.127, and the C'67, *BC* 9.33. See also the Preamble to the RCA *BCO*, p. 9, where it is stated: "The entire ministerial or pastoral office is summed up in Jesus Christ himself, in such a way that he is, in a sense, the only one holding that office." With the exception of the reference to C'67, these citations refer to the pastoral office; the principle expressed here, however, is applicable *mutatis mutandis* to every ministry in and through the church.

3. For the servant ministry see II HC, chaps. 18 and 16, *BC* 5.155, but also 5.114. C'67 speaks of the risen Christ as the savior of all persons and of those ". . . joined to him by faith . . . set right with God and commissioned to serve as his reconciling community" (*BC* 9.10); the Lutheran Confessions refer to ordained ministers as "church servants" (*Kirchendiener*). The 1970 LCA statement on the doctrine of the ministry, position statements, 1: "The Church exists to bring the grace of God in Jesus Christ to bear upon the whole of life. It is uniquely responsible for the redemptive relationship of faith to which all of its other concerns are subordinate, and it takes its place with other humanitarian servants to ameliorate the human situation." Cf. Preface, paragraphs 3 and 8, 1970 *LCA Minutes*, pp. 431f., 428f., 430.

4. "The life, death, resurrection, and promised coming of Jesus Christ has set the pattern for the church's mission. His life as man involves the church in the common life of men. His service to men commits the church to work for every form of human well-being. His suffering makes the church sensitive to all the sufferings of mankind so that it sees the face of Christ in the faces of men

in every kind of need. His crucifixion discloses to the church God's judgment on man's inhumanity to man and the awful consequences of its own complicity in injustice. In the power of the risen Christ and the hope of his coming the church sees the promise of God's renewal of man's life in society and God's victory over all wrong" C'67, *BC* 9.32. ALC "Definition of Terms" (for interpreting the constitution and bylaws, in *Handbook of the ALC*, 1983 ed., p. 12): "*Ministry*—The witness and service performed by this Church, its member congregations and their members in carrying out the mission given by Jesus Christ our Lord. *Mission*—The participation of the Church—its members, congregations, and other structures—in the redemptive work of the Triune God to bring wholeness to all persons, society, and his creation." LCA Constitution, Article V (Objects and Powers), section 1: "This church lives to be the instrument of the Holy Spirit in obedience to the commission of its Lord, and specifically a. To proclaim the Gospel through Word and Sacraments, to relate that Gospel to human need in every situation, and to extend the ministry of the Gospel to all the world. . . . h. To lift its voice in concord and to work in concert with forces for good, cooperating with church and other groups participating in activities that promote justice, relieve misery, and reconcile the estranged."

5. While the understanding of the prominence of the kingdom of God in the New Testament and its relationship to the church and God's mission in the world largely developed after the period when the confessional statements of the Reformation were written, these documents are not without a sense of the importance of the concept of the kingdom of God and the call of the church to mission. See, for example, WC, chaps. 25 and 35, *BC* 6.126 and 6.175; BelC, article 36; HCat, Q. 123, *BC* 4.123. For the kingdom in Lutheran documents of the sixteenth century: CA 17, *BkC* 38f.; Ap 7 and 8, 12–19, *BkC* 170f.; Ap 12, 176, *BkC* 210; and Ap 16, 2, *BkC* 222; SC, Creed, Second Article, *BkC* 345; LC, Lord's Prayer, Second Petition, sections 49–58, *BkC* 426–428.

6. "We believe that all members of the church are royal priests, enjoying full and free access to the throne of grace with no mediator save Jesus Christ. In calling a pastor to preach the Word of God and to administer the Sacraments in their midst and on their behalf, the members of a congregation exercise their royal priesthood and in no sense surrender it. The privilege and responsibility of ministering to the saints of God, of proclaiming his glory to all men, and of living victoriously in all the relationships of life, remain the privilege and responsibility of all members of the church." (From the ALC's *United Testimony on Faith and Life* [Part I, VI, *Handbook of the ALC*, 1983 ed., p. 153], an approved document between the uniting churches at their conventions in 1952, frequently referred to on matters of doctrine).

7. II HC seems to contradict the point made here when it insists that there is a distinction which must be drawn between the priesthood of all believers and ministry, the latter not being common to all Christians (*BC* 5.153). Ministry in this context refers to the pastoral office, and there is no intention here to

suggest that some Christians participate in no ministry. The Reformed Confessions, while not often employing the phrase "priesthood of all believers," make much of the Christian's responsibility to serve the neighbor. The ScotsC ties this to admission to the Lord's Table (chap. 23, *BC* 3.23); cf. II HC, article 16, *BC* 5.114; see also the explications of the commandments in several of the Reformed Confessions. In the Lutheran Confessions the concept of the priesthood of all believers appears but only obliquely. To the church corporately, which is the royal priesthood instituted by God, has been given the gospel or the keys; therefore, "the church retains the right of electing and ordaining ministers" (Melanchthon's "Treatise on the Power and Primacy of the Pope," section 72, cf. 60–72 and 24, *BkC* 332, cf. 330–32 and 324). The ALC's *United Testimony on Faith and Life*, Part II, II, pp. 7–8 (*Handbook of the ALC*, 1983 ed., pp. 155–57) directly addresses the relation of the priesthood of believers and the public office of the ministry.

"The church will not restrain but will rather encourage all its members to private study of the Word of God; to bear Christian witness in word and in deed; to seek opportunities for mutual edification; to share in the teaching ministry, locally and in the church at large, when requested through regular channels; and to accept the responsibility of public proclamation of the Word when appointed to do so by the properly constituted authority of the congregation or of the church body" (from the ALC's *United Testimony on Faith and Life*, Part II, II [*Handbook of the ALC*, 1983 ed., p. 157], p. 9, an approved document between the uniting churches at their conventions in 1952, frequently referred to on matters of doctrine).

The Cambridge Platform (p. 208) speaks of a "mutual covenant" grounded "in the promises of Christ's special presence in the church: whence they have fellowship with him, and in him one with another" (p. 209).

8. It is interesting to note that while the Lutheran confessional statements of the sixteenth century abound in references to the doctrine of Christian vocation, the Confessions of the Reformed Reformation are silent on this matter, e.g., CA 26, *BkC* 65; CA 27, *BkC* 72–73; Ap 27, *BkC* 275; Ap 23, *BkC* 244; Ap 15, *BkC* 219. The silence of the Reformed Confessions on Christian vocation does not stem from an understanding that differs from the Lutheran. By the time the "second generation" of the Reformation had appeared on the scene, it was no longer necessary to assert this doctrine; it was assumed. There is mention of the doctrine in II HC, 19, *BC* 5.250; cf. C'67, *BC* 9.35–38.

Limited in scope though it was, the early congregationalist understanding of the ministry of the laity was strong. From the Cambridge Platform (p. 209) a fairly consistent line can be drawn to the present emphasis in the UCC on "the ministry of the laity" (*Minutes/Thirteenth General Synod/United Church of Christ*, 27 June–1 July 1981, p. 53).

9. There is no question that both the Reformed and Lutheran Confessions of the Reformation period called for a "set-apart" pastoral office. For Reformed references see: BelC, article 31; II HC, 18, *BC* 5.142–43; WC, chaps. 14 and 25, *BC* 6.070 and 6.127. The Lutheran Ap 13, 12f., speaks plainly on this: "The

church has the command to appoint ministers; to this we must subscribe wholeheartedly, for we know that God approves this ministry and is present in it. It is good to extol the ministry of the Word with every possible kind of praise . . . ." (*BkC* 212). More colorfully, from the preface to Luther's LC, section 6: "Indeed, even among the nobility there are some louts and skinflints who declare that we can do without pastors and preachers from now on because we have everything in books and can learn it all by ourselves. So they blithely let parishes fall into decay . . . ." (*BkC* 359). These two quotations may be allowed to speak for the host of references to the necessity of the pastoral office in the Lutheran Confessions.

10. The necessity of a pastoral office is clearly taught in the Confessions of the Reformation; the form of that office, however, is not presented as a confessional matter.

11. Both Lutheran and Reformed Confessions teach that the authority of the pastoral office derives from the Lord, or the Word; cf. II HC, chap. 18, *BC* 5.165, for example, with Ap 28, 18, *BkC* 284.

Cambridge Platform (p. 209) sees the ministerial office derived from the Lord Jesus Christ as the *supreme* power in the church.

12. The churches of both traditions have since the time of the Reformation ordained their ministers in a rite which included the laying on of hands. "And those who are elected are to be ordained . . . with public prayer and laying on of hands" (II HC, chap. 18, *BC* 5.151; cf. C'67, *BC* 9.39). From the SA 3, 10, 3: "Accordingly, as we are taught by the examples of the ancient churches and Fathers, we shall and ought ourselves ordain suitable persons to this office" (*BkC* 314). See also Ap 13, 7–13, where ordination (with the laying on of hands) is presented in relation to the ministry of the Word (*BkC* 212).

For the teachings of the Lutheran Confessions concerning the apostolicity of the pastoral office, see Ap 28, 18, *BkC*, p. 284; "Treatise on the Power and Primacy of the Pope," section 26, where, commenting on Matt. 16:18, Melanchthon states: "Besides, the ministry of the New Testament is not bound to place and persons, as the Levitical priesthood is, but is spread abroad through the whole world and exists wherever God gives his gifts, apostles, prophets, pastors, teachers. Nor is this ministry valid because of any individual's authority but because of the Word given by Christ" (*BkC* 324); Ap 7 and 8, 28, *BkC* 173. For the Reformed confessional statements: II HC, chap. 18, *BC* 5.147; HCat, Questions 83–85, *BC* 4.083–85; II HC, chap. 14, *BC* 5.096.

Consistently from the Cambridge Platform (ordination by "imposition of hands," p. 215) to the UCC *Constitution and Bylaws* (setting "apart by prayer and the laying on of hands," p. 5), there has been the same understanding of the rite of ordination.

13. For a description of office, ordination, and oversight in the Reformed tradition, see the essay, "Office and Ordination in the Reformed Tradition," by Paul R. Fries, which is found in Appendix 6.

14. It is remarkable that the question of oversight, which occasioned extensive discussion in the Lutheran confessional statements, receives so little com-

ment in those of the Reformed tradition. References in the Lutheran *BkC* are so numerous that they need not be listed here. The II HC does state: "Nevertheless, for the sake of preserving order some one of the ministers called the assembly together, proposed matters to be laid before it, gathered the opinions of the others, in short, to the best of man's ability took precaution lest any confusion should arise." Thus, the II HC concludes, order is to be preserved (chap. 18, *BC* 5.161). In the Reformed tradition the form which oversight takes has rarely been a confessional issue.

Depending on what one means by "oversight," it is fair to say that in the Congregationalist strand of the United Church of Christ the form oversight takes has constantly been a "confessional" issue.

15. Today it is only in Hungary that the Reformed Church has bishops.

16. "Christian faith *seeks* fellowship, that is, the discovery and the practice of this spiritual fellowship with other Christians. It laments isolation; it yearns for communion. Christian faith seeks fellowship in prayer, in corporate worship, in the Communion, in doing the Lord's work, and even in suffering for the faith" (from the ALC's *United Testimony on Faith and Life*, Part II, VI [*Handbook of the ALC*, 1983 ed., p. 161], p. 2, an approved document between the united churches at their conventions in 1952, frequently referred to on matters of doctrine).

# APPENDIXES

APPENDIX 1

# MARBURG REVISITED* LUTHERAN-REFORMED CONSULTATION SERIES, 1962–1966

## PREFACE

Early in this decade the desirability of theological conversations between members of the Lutheran and the Reformed traditions was discussed informally. In the spring of 1961 sponsorship of such conversations was approved by the North American Area of the World Alliance of Reformed Churches Holding the Presbyterian Order and the U.S.A. National Committee of the Lutheran World Federation. A preliminary meeting was held in New York in February, 1962; annual consultations thereafter culminated in a meeting at Princeton, New Jersey in February, 1966, when the sessions were given over chiefly to summarizing and evaluating the previous discussions.

It was agreed that the objective would be "to explore the theological relations between the Lutheran and Reformed churches to discover to what extent the differences which have divided these communions in the past still constitute obstacles to mutual understanding." In order to encompass the concerns of groups within the two traditions not related to the two sponsoring organizations, invitations were extended to and accepted by the Orthodox Presbyterian Church, the Christian Reformed Church, and the Lutheran Church—Missouri Synod to take part. It was clear from the start that the individuals named to participate would speak for themselves, their conclusions neither necessarily representing nor binding the respective churches which appointed them.

The papers and summaries prepared in connection with each annual consultation were printed in pamphlet form and given wide distribution among the clergy of the related church bodies in this country and Canada. The recommendation that this material be made available for use in theological seminaries led to the decision to have them printed together in a single volume.

The statement drawn up and unanimously approved at the final session is ample evidence that these theological conversations were fruitful. Although all discussions were "off the record" and it is not always

**Marburg Revisited: A Reexamination of Lutheran and Reformed Traditions*, ed. Paul C. Empie and James I. McCord (Minneapolis: Augsburg Publishing House, 1966).

easy to relate the summary statements to the papers discussed prior to their formulation, it can be said that as the participants became better acquainted and more effective in communication, caricatures disappeared and misunderstandings were rectified. Most important of all, distinctions were made between differences which were matters of relative emphases rather than contradictions in substance. Not all controversial points were touched upon nor were all differences resolved. However, the conclusion that each group recognized in the other a true understanding of the Gospel is significant and the implications of this fact are inescapable.

We suggest that the materials in this book be read in the light of the following statement adopted by participants in their final session:

> During these four meetings we have examined carefully the major issues which have aroused theological controversy between our traditions for generations past. At some points we have discovered that our respective views of each other have been inherited caricatures initially caused by misunderstanding or polemical zeal.
>
> In other instances it has become apparent that efforts to guard against possible distortions of truth have resulted in varying emphases in related doctrines which are not in themselves contradictory and in fact are complementary, and which are viewed in a more proper balance in our contemporary theological formulations.
>
> A number of differing views and emphases remain to be resolved, but we are encouraged to believe that further contacts will lead to further agreement between the churches here represented. We regard none of these remaining differences to be of sufficient consequence to prevent fellowship. We have recognized in each other's teachings a common understanding of the Gospel and have concluded that the issues which divided the two major branches of the Reformation can no longer be regarded as constituting obstacles to mutual understanding and fellowship.
>
> We are grateful to God that he brought us together for these discussions, acknowledging that such confrontation under the guidance of the Holy Spirit was long overdue. Although we can speak only for ourselves, we express our conviction that the work begun in this way must not be permitted to lapse, but should be carried on to fruition by the churches we represent.
>
> We who have had the privilege during the course of these conversations of strengthening the bonds of Christian unity and brotherly affection thank God for the evident working of his spirit in our midst and pray that what was begun in this way will be carried on to a successful conclusion with all "deliberate speed."

James I. McCord, President
Princeton Theological Seminary

Paul C. Empie, Executive Director
National Lutheran Council

## SUMMARY STATEMENT ON GOSPEL, CONFESSION AND SCRIPTURE

1. Both Lutheran and Reformed churches are evangelical in the sense that they are rooted in, live by, proclaim and confess the gospel of the saving act of God in Jesus Christ. They receive it as it is revealed in the prophetic and apostolic scriptures, attested through the witness of the Holy Spirit, and preserved in the tradition of the catholic faith as expressed in the commonly accepted creeds of the ancient church.

2. The churches of the Reformation confessed this gospel by means of the biblical concept of justification by grace through faith alone. The scriptures also present the same gospel in other concepts, such as reconciliation, regeneration, and redemption. An evangelical confession accordingly may be, and has been, framed in terms of one or more of these.

3. We are agreed that the new life of faith in Christ involves obedience, but there is some question concerning the place and meaning of law in the new life.

4. The Church is constrained by the gospel to confess its faith. Such confession takes the primary form of praise to God. It must also take the form of confession before man, testimony to and defense of the gospel in various historical situations.

5. Confession takes a variety of forms both in scripture and in the Church. The history of the Church exhibits such types as the doxological confession which celebrates the glory of the gospel, the kerygmatic which identifies and declares the gospel, the catechetical which serves for the instruction of believers, and the critical which distinguishes the gospel from errors and misunderstandings.

6. The confessions originated in different geographical and historical situations and they use different vocabularies. These differences do not of themselves preclude unity in the faith which is confessed in them.

7. Credal and confessional subscription is regarded seriously in both Lutheran and Reformed churches, but there is some diversity of opinion concerning its meaning.

8. We are agreed that in the canonical scriptures of the Old and New Testaments the acts of God which culminate in the revelation of Himself in Jesus Christ, His Son our Lord, are set forth by chosen witnesses under the leading of the Holy Spirit.

9. The confessions affirm the supreme authority of scripture as the norm for the proclamation of the gospel and provide authoritative guidance and direction in the interpretation of this normative scripture.

## SUMMARY STATEMENT ON CHRISTOLOGY, THE LORD'S SUPPER AND ITS OBSERVANCE IN THE CHURCH

1. In the present situation, in which windows are opening between Protestants and Roman Catholics as well as between Protestants and Eastern Orthodox, it is especially important that Lutheran and Reformed churches appreciate and bear witness to their common evangelical heritage in the Reformation.

2. We acknowledge the abiding significance of the recovery of the gospel granted to our churches in the Reformation. We confess that this gospel imposes on us the necessity of constant re-examination of our theological-formulations in the light of the word of God.

3. During the Reformation both Reformed and Lutheran churches exhibited an evangelical intention when they understood the Lord's Supper in the light of the saving act of God in Christ. Despite this common intention, different terms and concepts were employed which not only shared in the inadequacy of all human thought and language but also led to mutual misunderstanding and misrepresentation. Properly interpreted, the differing terms and concepts were often complementary rather than contradictory.

4. In the last four centuries both Lutheran and Reformed churches tended to be one-sided in their teaching and practice. Unfortunately, they did not support or correct one another as they might have done if they had mutually recognized how much they had in common.

5. Ever since the sixteenth century Reformed and Lutheran churches have held the conviction that the same gift is offered in the preached word and in the administered sacrament. Each of these is both word and deed, for in preaching word is action and in the Lord's Supper action is word.

6. When by word is meant the proclamation of the gospel, the sacrament is a form of visible, enacted word through which Christ and his saving benefits are effectively offered to men. Accordingly, the sacrament is a means of peace.

The assurance of his presence is given in the self-witness of Christ in the instituting rite: This is my body, this is my blood. The realization of his presence in the sacrament is effected by the Holy Spirit through the word.

We are agreed that the sacrament does not simply serve to confirm a faith that is awakened by preaching: it also arouses faith through its presentation of the gospel.

7. An adequate doctrine of the Lord's Supper requires some reference to sacrifice. The perfect self-offering of the Son of God is the atoning sacrifice whereby our self-offering to God in worship and in loving gift to the neighbor is made possible and acceptable.

8. We are agreed that the presence of Christ in the sacrament is not effected by faith but acknowledged by faith. The worthy participant is the one who receives in faith and repentance the Christ who offers himself in the sacrament. The unworthy participant is the one who fails to acknowledge the Lordship of Christ, his presence in the sacrament, and the fellowship of the brethren in the common Lord. Such unworthy participation brings judgment.

9. The significance of christology for the Lord's Supper is that it provides assurance that it is the total Christ, the divine-human person, who is present in the sacrament, but it does not explain how he is present.

10. Our churches are not in full agreement on the practice of intercommunion because they hold different views of the relation of doctrine to the unity of the Church.

## SUMMARY STATEMENT ON CREATION AND REDEMPTION, LAW AND GOSPEL, JUSTIFICATION AND SANCTIFICATION

1. The Reformed and Lutheran traditions are agreed that creation is the work of God, the Father, Son, and Holy Spirit, and that, therefore, the creation is essentially good in spite of the presence and power of evil.

2. The God who creates also redeems and for this reason the creation must be understood in the light of redemption and redemption in the context of creation.

3. Some in our traditions tend to relate redemption too narrowly to man as sinner. We, however, are agreed that we should also bear adequate witness to the significance of redemption for the whole created order, inasmuch as creation and redemption have an eschatological dimension pointing to a new heaven and a new earth.

4. We observe that with respect to law and gospel there are different emphases in our traditions. In part these differences were and are semantic and arise out of different patterns of theological thought. For example, the Lutheran description of law as "always accusing" (*Apology IV*, 38) restricts the meaning of the term "law" more severely than

is the case either in the totality of scripture or in the Calvinistic tradition.

5. We are agreed both that Jesus Christ is the fulfillment and end of the law, and that in the Christian life God continues to lay his claim upon the redeemed; but we are not agreed how to denominate that claim, whether law or gospel. Both Calvinists and Lutherans know themselves to be saved through the gospel and called to Christian obedience.

6. We are agreed that the doctrine of justification by faith is fundamental in both traditions. We recognize, however, that for Lutherans this doctrine has played a more formative role in the articulation of theology. This difference is due in part to the historical situations in which Luther and Calvin did their theological work.

7. We are agreed that each tradition has sought to preserve the wholeness of the gospel as including the forgiveness of sins and the renewal of life. Our discussions have revealed that justification and sanctification have been distinguished from each other and related to each other in rather different ways in our traditions.

8. Failure properly to interpret and relate justification and sanctification leads to the development of antinomian and legalistic distortions in both traditions.

In the light of these observations we acknowledge that differences exist between us, but we record our gratitude to God for the progress we have made toward mutual understanding and resolution of our differences. We also acknowledge the obligation laid upon us to submit ourselves to the guidance of the Word and Spirit in the further pursuit of these objectives.

## SUMMARY STATEMENT ON ETHICS AND ETHOS— CHRISTIAN SERVICE IN THE MODERN WORLD

1. We are agreed that there is a common evangelical basis for Christian ethics in the theology of the Reformers. Both the Lutheran and the Reformed traditions have emphasized the new obedience of Christians through faith active in love and the inseparability of justification and sanctification. Our dialogue leads us to conclude that differing formulations of the relation between law and gospel were prompted by a common concern to combat the errors of legalism on the one hand and antinomianism on the other. While there remains a difference among us as to the importance we attach to the need for the instruction of

God's law in the Christian life, we do not regard this as a divisive issue. We affirm together that Christians are free from the bondage of the law in order to live in love under the direction of God's Word and Spirit to the end of good order and eternal life.

2. In attempting to translate Reformation theology into the twentieth century, however, we must take into account not only a clericalism that frustrates the ministry of the laity, but also a secularism which denies that the world is the creation of God and the object of his love. This world is the arena for Christian ethical service. The impersonal structures of power in modern society are morally ambiguous. While they tend to pervert the humanity of men and the proper use of things, they also offer untold possibilities for good. This situation compels us to search for new ways of loving our neighbors. Recent technological and sociological developments intensify the urgency for translating personal love into social justice.

3. We believe that faithful obedience in modern life involves renewed stress on the vital interaction of Christian righteousness and civil righteousness. In response to the gospel of Christ, we welcome the opportunity for a united witness through Christian social action in service to the world. Such responsible public action will also involve us in cooperation with men of good will who are likewise committed to peace, freedom and justice in society.

## CONFESSIONAL INTEGRITY AND ECUMENICAL DIALOGUE

WARREN A. QUANBECK

Conversations between denominational families always raise questions and sometimes also suspicions about the thoroughness and loyalty of the proceedings. If differences could not be resolved in the 16th and 17th centuries, when the very survival of the Reformation seemed to hang upon some kind of agreement, why should they be easier to resolve in the present day? When those taking part in the discussion announce that they see no insurmountable barrier separating Reformed and Lutheran churches, journalists rejoice at the prospect of a good story, but doctrinal loyalists on both sides harbor suspicions. They suspect that the real issues were not faced squarely, or that formulas have been devised which pretend agreement but which only conceal deep differences, or that one side in the discussion has simply given in to the other. Is it possible for Reformed and Lutheran theologians, in full loyalty to their respective traditions, to face the issues which have separated them for centuries and reach profound and genuine agreement?

It is important to recognize that this is a possibility in our day, not because theologians are willing to betray their confessional heritage, or because they are skillful in contriving deceptive formulas of agreement, but because the whole theological scenery has been transformed through a tremendous growth in knowledge and through changes in theological perspective which have developed in the last century and a half. The development of empirical method in the natural and historical sciences, which began in the Renaissance, has in modern times produced profound changes in the way we ask questions, in the way we experience reality and in the way we understand ourselves and our relation to the world. It has greatly expanded the amount of knowledge we have of the world and our past and at the same time given deeper insight into the complexity of human problems. Man's scientific horizon has been expanded outward in a remarkable way through the replacement of a Ptolemaic world view by the Copernican outlook. Our knowledge of the past has been enriched in a corresponding way through historical research. The sciences of anthropology, psychology, sociology and others have presented us with an immensely detailed knowledge of human life and culture in a great number of different settings. From this information we have come to recognize the fact of cultural differentiation: that different cultures view the world and human experience in different ways and express their apprehension of life in different conceptual frameworks. This has led to a deepened understanding of languages in human life and thought and the realization that there is not simply one human way of thinking and speaking, but that even with a single linguistic tradition there are multiple languages corresponding to man's different ways of apprehending and reacting to his environment.

These developments have immensely enriched and complicated the task of theological reflection but they have also provided perspectives from which traditional questions appear in a new light. This does not mean that we are automatically wiser than our forefathers, but only that we have the same task in a quite different situation. They attempted to make the gospel meaningful for their time; our task is to communicate the gospel in an age of science, secular humanism and universal culture. The gospel remains the same, and the missionary responsibility of the church is the same, but the change in situation imposes upon us the task of using our resources to confront our contemporaries with the gospel. Let us examine some of the ways in which the changes in our cultural situation affect the traditional differences between Reformed and Lutheran theologies.

1. The development of modern historical science has given us a new way of apprehending both past and present. Whereas an older way of thought saw the world and man himself as something given, complete and essentially unchanging, we today see our experience in developmental terms. We see the world not as a static essence, but as a process of development. We see man and human institutions as products of a past and processes of development in the present—growing, maturing, declining, dying. We can only understand man, an institution or an artifact, in relation to the culture in which it exists, and to ignore this social, historical and cultural situation is to forego understanding.

This has important consequences for our understanding of the bible. The exegete of the Middle Ages would treat the bible as though it has no historical context, and apply texts immediately to his problems without attempting to understand them in the situation out of which they developed. When this method involved him in interpretative difficulties, he could escape into spiritualizing interpretations, invoking the tropological, allegorical or analogical sense of the passage. Today we cannot profitably or honestly ignore the historical context from which the books of the bible have emerged, and when we cannot be sure of this context, as happens, for example, in certain psalms, we find ourselves in interpretative difficulties. We can only understand what a text says to us when we understand what it meant to its first readers. This does not mean that all older commentaries are useless, for the best interpreters of the bible, Augustine, Luther, Calvin and others, brought great theological insight to bear on the problems of interpretation, and frequently operate in historical categories. But their work must be critically examined, and it sometimes turns out that their theological insight was better than their exegesis. Luther's understanding of the Lord's Supper, for example, shows insight which anticipates much laboriously achieved modern understanding of scripture, although a modern exegete would have a difficult time defending some of the exegetical scaffolding by which he supports and defends his position. Or in examining a dogmatic treatise we may agree with the theological assertion which is made even though we conclude that many passages of scripture assembled to support it have nothing to do with the question.

The historical-critical approach to the scriptures is not something to be opposed, rejected, or merely tolerated; it is a necessity of modern biblical study, and without it, it is more difficult for us to hear the word of God in the scriptures. The wrong use of the method should not lead to condemnation of the method, but rather a correction of a poor methodology. The method itself is one of God's gifts to his church in modern times; many contemporary students have learned that its proper use enables them to hear God speaking in the bible.

The awareness of historical development also has important consequences for our understanding of the history of theology. In its light we can see clearly that the Nicene Creed uses the theological method and vocabulary of the 4th century to assert the truth about Jesus Christ and to reject misunderstandings of his person and mission which threatened the clarity and power of the gospel. The language of the creed is not biblical language, but that of fourth century philosophy. Those who drew up the creed were compelled to use non-biblical language to assert the truth of the biblical message. We grasp what was at issue at Nicea as we use historical scholarship to understand the terminology used by the contending parties, to comprehend the issues in dispute, and so to understand how the church defended the true proclamation of the gospel against perversions. When we become familiar with the methods of historical scholarship we recognize that no theological vocabulary can be absolutized; each vocabulary has arisen in a specific situation for a special task and can only be understood in its situation. The task of theology is not simply to repeat the words which have proven effective in proclaiming or defending the gospel in past situations, but to understand the gospel so that we can do in our day what other theologians have done in the past. In fact, the process of repeating theological formulas can communicate a wrong understanding of the gospel if the meaning of the words has changed or the situation is altered. To repeat theological expressions addressed to humanistic optimism in a situation of despair about human capacities may not produce a repentance leading to life but only deepen a sorrow leading to death. And to proclaim to incorrigible optimists the encouraging words properly addressed to those in despair may not lead them to the true evaluation of the human predicament.

The problem of man is also illuminated by an historically informed theology. The static, essentialist theology had great difficulty doing justice to the biblical understanding of man in society or to the eschatological dimensions of the gospel. It tended to speak of man in individualistic terms, overlooking the meaning of the biblical expression "in Adam" as a collective existence under judgment, and doing less than justice to the new life in Christ as life in the people of God, the body of Christ, the new humanity. Its static terminology was also inadequate to express the dynamic tension of the Christian life between the resurrection of Christ and his *parousia.* The recovery of dynamic and eschatological language has enabled theologians to relate more effectively to the view of man expressed by modern anthropologists, sociologists and psychologists and thus to enter into a real exchange of ideas and genuine discussion and not be imprisoned in an ecclesiastical monologue.

In brief, the historical-developmental way of thinking gives the theologian tools which enable him to understand the scriptures and the history of theology more effectively, and also give him a standpoint to enter into a real discussion with contemporary thinking about man and his problems. This does not mean that the theological work of earlier times is without value and must be discarded. The worth of the earlier work becomes especially clear when it is studied historically. In this way the purpose and religious concerns of earlier theologians become available to illuminate our theological tasks and to give us the benefit of their wisdom and insight, even though we must learn to express it in contemporary vocabulary if it is to be meaningful for us or others of our time. The love of God in Christ remains the same, human estrangement in sin continues to be a constant, but the specific shape of man's flight from God varies from culture to culture. It is this varying form of man's evasion of God which sets the theological task: to recognize what tactics contemporary man uses to hide from God and to find the language which can communicate the judgment and love of God to him in his hiding place. The problems of theology have a certain consistency from age to age, and yet the shift from substantialist, static thinking to developmental dynamic categories means that every problem appears in a new light and from a different perspective.

2. A second way in which the historical development of theology has altered the setting and treatment of traditional questions is in the immense amount of new knowledge at the disposal of contemporary thought. The last century has witnessed a kind of explosion of knowledge so that the amount of material to be mastered in every branch of theology has greatly increased. Both in our knowledge of the scriptures and of the history of theology new dimensions of material are now available. It now appears that the different positions taken by Calvinist and Lutheran theologies are not always at odds with each other, but often represent different but complementary accents, different approaches which are both needed for a grasp of the fulness of the problem.

One example can be seen in the differing confessional histories of the churches. They differ from each other not as two answers to the same problems in arithmetic, one of which can be shown to be right and the other wrong, but as two different methods or styles of writing confessions. The Augsburg Confession of 1530 shows the church of the Reformation relating herself to the ancient Catholic tradition, and concerned to assert that what the reformers teach is no innovation but the true Catholic heritage. It is confession in the primary biblical sense of the word, the praise of God in the heralding forth of his mighty saving deeds. It points to the great primal realities of the Christian tradition and calls attention to the way God has acted for human salvation in Christ, and how he continues to act in the life and witness of his church. The Reformed Confessions, on the other hand, come from a later period in the life of the Reformation, in which the break with Rome is now taken for granted, and the churches of the Reformation seek to identify themselves. They are not as doxological in character as the Augsburg Confession, but are more dogmatic. They reflect the changed situation in the second generation of the Reformation, where the concern is less identification with the Catholic tradition than with the differentiation of one theological position over against another.

The development of an ecumenical approach to theology has also been aided by the increased amount of historical information available. When theology is concerned with only one church tradition, it can easily become narrow, defensive, and apologetic. But where it is exposed to a wide range of traditions, and sees them in historical perspective, it can no longer limit itself to justification of a single tradition, but must deal responsibly with the entire range of Christian churches. To the extent that its reading of other traditions is sympathetic and imaginative it discovers theological concerns similar to its own and also emphases which complement and occasionally correct elements in its own tradition. As it develops self confidence it finds less necessity for defending every event in its own denominational history, can acknowledge that the gospel has not always been expounded in its fulness, and can recognize and appreciate the presence of Christ in other traditions as well.

This induces a new theological mood. The task of the theologian is seen not as that of attorney for his own ecclesiastical institution, who must at all costs score points for his side in the theological debate. It is rather seen as responsibility to the whole gospel, and the ability to recognize both the strengths and the weaknesses of one's own tradition. The theological discussion also changes, becoming more a joint search for the truth of the gospel than an attempt to justify one's own side. It lays heavy demands upon those who take part in such discussion. It requires that they know the scriptures, that they are informed about the history of the church, the development of theology, and the situation which the church confronts today. It demands maturity, poise and self-confidence to avoid the perils of defensiveness and self-righteousness. It presupposes openness to the truth, and a willingness to have one's understanding of the gospel deepened and enriched by encounter with representatives of other traditions.

The discussion of the doctrine of the Lord's Supper is an especially good illustration of the benefits of an historically informed study proceeding under ecumenical auspices. The historical study of the scriptures and of the development of eucharistic doctrine has shown how rich and complex the Christian tradition is at this point. Each of the great traditions has developed one aspect of the biblical witness and worked out its implications for the whole of Christian doctrine, for worship, and for service. Other elements have not usually been excluded, but have not been worked out with the same thoroughness.

When the traditions are set alongside each other and examined in a sympathetic way, it can be seen that one does not necessarily have to choose one doctrinal tradition to the exclusion of all others. To be a loyal Lutheran does not mean that one can see no value in the dogmatic or liturgical tradition of the Eastern Orthodox churches, or that one must condemn the total doctrinal statement of the Roman Catholic or Calvinist traditions. The New Testament witnesses to a rich variety of theological motifs in interpreting the Lord's Supper: memorial, communion, thanksgiving, sacrifice, mystery, anticipation. No tradition in the church has done justice to them all; each tradition has sought to develop one or more of them. What is seen in the study of the scriptures, and noted again in the development of the church's doctrine, becomes real and existential in ecumenical discussion. Here one can see how Thomas Aquinas and John Calvin strive to assert the same religious concerns, how Luther's profound sacramental realism can be complemented by Calvin's stress upon the Holy Spirit, how the entire Western tradition can learn from a study of Eastern Orthodox theology and spirituality. As we perceive the richness and diversity of the church's tradition rooted in the scriptures we begin to see the dimensions of our theological task. We need a more thorough knowledge of the scriptures, an ever deepened understanding of the development of doctrine, and a sensitivity growing out of experience which enables us to recognize the significance of doctrine for worship, fellowship, service and mission.

## REPORT TO THE SPONSORING CONFESSIONAL ORGANIZATIONS

1. We believe that the work assigned to us, namely: "to explore the theological relations between the Lutheran and Reformed churches to discover to what extent differences which have divided these communions in the past still constitute obstacles to mutual understanding," has been completed, that the conversations have been fruitful, and that additional meetings of this group are not necessary.

2. We recommend that the several judicatories of our respective groups be encouraged to

   a. Sponsor a series of Lutheran-Reformed study groups in various strategic geographical areas, using the four publications growing out of our work as background information and guides, and involving members of the Lutheran-Reformed theological discussion group, and other selected theologians and pastors as resource persons.

   b. Make these four publications available to all the theological seminaries of our two traditions, urging them to make use of these materials in an appropriate course or courses.

3. We recommend that full publicity be given to the findings of these consultations and to their implications for the life of our churches today.

4. As a result of our studies and discussions we see no insuperable obstacles to pulpit and altar fellowship and, therefore, we recommend to our parent bodies that they encourage their constituent churches to enter into discussions looking forward to intercommunion and the fuller recognition of one another's ministries.

## PARTICIPANTS

**Representing the Lutheran Tradition:**

Dr. Conrad Bergendoff, President Emeritus, Augustana College, Rock Island, Illinois
Dr. Herbert J. A. Bouman, Concordia Seminary, St. Louis, Missouri
Dr. George W. Forell, State University of Iowa, Iowa City, Iowa
Dr. Martin H. Franzman, Concordia Seminary, St. Louis, Missouri
Dr. Martin J. Heinecken, Lutheran Theological Seminary, Philadelphia, Pennsylvania
Dr. William H. Narum, St. Olaf College, Northfield, Minnesota
Dr. Warren A. Quanbeck, Luther Seminary, Saint Paul, Minnesota

Dr. Theodore G. Tappert, Lutheran Theological Seminary, Philadelphia, Pennsylvania

**Alternates:**

Dr. Paul M. Bretscher, Concordia Seminary, St. Louis, Missouri
Dr. Harold Ditmanson, St. Olaf College, Northfield, Minnesota
Dr. William H. Lazareth, Lutheran Theological Seminary, Philadelphia, Pennsylvania
Dr. Fred W. Meuser, Evangelical Lutheran Theological Seminary, Columbus, Ohio

**Consultants:**

Dr. Paul C. Empie, Executive Director, National Lutheran Council (U.S.A. National Committee, Lutheran World Federation), New York, New York
Dr. Virgil R. Westlund, Secretary, Department of Theological Cooperation, National Lutheran Council, New York, New York

**Representing the Reformed Tradition:**

Dr. William Fennell, Emmanuel College, Toronto, Ontario, Canada
Dr. Howard G. Hageman, Minister, North Reformed Dutch Church, Newark, New Jersey
Dr. David Hay, Knox College, Toronto, Ontario, Canada
Dr. George S. Hendry, Princeton Theological Seminary, Princeton, New Jersey
Dr. John Leith, Union Theological Seminary, Richmond, Virginia
Dr. Henry Stob, Calvin College, Grand Rapids, Michigan
Dr. Bard Thompson, Drew University, Madison, New Jersey
Dr. Cornelius Van Til, Westminster Theological Seminary, Philadelphia, Pennsylvania

**Alternates:**

Prof. Robert C. Johnson, Yale Divinity School, New Haven, Connecticut
Prof. Joseph McLelland, McGill University, Montreal, Quebec, Canada

**Consultant:**

Dr. James I. McCord, North American Secretary, World Alliance of Reformed Churches/World Presbyterian Alliance, Princeton, New Jersey

## APPENDIX 2

# LUTHERAN-REFORMED CONSULTATION SERIES II, 1972–1974

### I

The first round of Lutheran-Reformed conversations was held from 1962 to 1966 and resulted in the publication of *Marburg Revisited: A Reexamination of Lutheran and Reformed Traditions.*[1] It covered gospel, confession and scripture; the Lord's Supper and christology; justification and sanctification; law and gospel; creation and redemption; and ethics. A summary statement followed each of the four sections, setting forth the consensus and remaining differences. In spite of important differences, on the basis of the consensus arrived at the group reported to the sponsoring confessional organizations (i.e., the North American Area of the World Alliance of Reformed Churches and the U.S.A. National Committee of the Lutheran World Federation) as follows: "As a result of our studies and discussions we see no insuperable obstacles to pulpit and altar fellowship and, therefore, we recommend to our parent bodies that they encourage their constituent churches to enter into discussions looking forward to intercommunion and the fuller recognition of one another's ministries."[2] Although *Marburg Revisited* was sent to the constituent churches, no official action was taken by any Reformed or Lutheran church "to enter into discussions looking forward to intercommunion and the fuller recognition of one another's ministries."[3]

1. In the remit for the second round of conversations, drawn up in July 1971 by the presidents of the church bodies participating in the Lutheran Council in the U.S.A., and by stated clerks of churches of the North American Area of the World Alliance of Reformed Churches (Presbyterian and Congregational), it was stated: "In resuming the Lutheran-Reformed conversations, it shall be the objective to assess the consensus and remaining differences in the theology and life of the participating churches as they bear upon the teaching of the Gospel in the current situation." It was our aim in these discussions to test and deepen this consensus in the current situation without ignoring remaining differences. Although the remit focused on "the teaching of

the Gospel in the current situation, the results of the *Marburg Revisited* study regarding intercommunion, and recent developments affecting church relationships, brought us repeatedly back to problems of pulpit and altar fellowship. It became apparent to us that attention would have to be given to the sources of the diversity of theological understanding and to the differences of ecclesiastical life style that play into the separation between Lutheran and Reformed churches. It also became clear to us that some of the most intransigent theological differences run across denominational lines.

2. Representatives designated by the presidents of the church bodies participating in LCUSA and the North American Area of the WARC held six meetings from 1972 to 1974. Papers were read and discussed on (1) Churches in Dialogue Today; (2) *Marburg Revisited;* (3) the Leuenberg Agreement of 1973; and (4) the official positions of the participating churches on matters of fellowship. At the first meeting in Princeton, New Jersey, 14–15 April 1972, papers were presented by Dr. William Weiblen on "The Church in Dialogue in 1972," with a response by Dr. Thomas Parker; by Dr. Daniel Migliore on "An American Looks at Leuenberg" with a response by Dr. George Forell; and Drs. Ralph Bohlmann and John Leith on "*Marburg Revisited* in the Light of 1972."

At the fall meeting in Chicago eight brief papers were read by Drs. Arnold Carlson and Thomas Parker on "Leuenberg's Hermeneutics and Theological Methodology"; by Drs. Henry Stob and James Burtness on "The Understanding of the Gospel in the Leuenberg Agreement"; by Drs. M. Eugene Osterhaven and James Burtness on "Problem Areas: Are Past Differences Still Issues?"; and by Drs. Eugene Klug and Roger Hazleton on "Achieving Church Fellowship."

At the spring meeting of 1973 in New York papers were presented by Dr. Walter Wietzke on "Identity and Identification" with a response by Dr. Daniel Migliore; by Dr. Robert Paul on "The Table of the Lord" with a response by Dr. Ralph Bohlmann; and a discussion was led by Professor Peter Berger on sociological issues in the Protestant churches in America.

At the fall meeting in 1973 in Grand Rapids, Michigan, representatives of the participating churches presented papers on their churches' official positions with respect to: (1) requirements for admission to the Lord's Table and to pulpits; (2) the role of the Eucharist in the life of the church, with special attention to its juridical and disciplinary functions, and its relation to other doctrines; (3) ways to overcome obstacles to fellowship. The representatives who presented papers were Drs. Howard Tepker (The Lutheran Church—Missouri Synod), George Forell (Lutheran Church in America), William Weiblen (The American Lutheran Church), Henry Stob (Christian Reformed Church), Eugene Osterhaven (Reformed Church in America), John Leith (Presbyterian Church in the United States), Thomas Parker (United Presbyterian Church in the U.S.A.), and Roger Hazleton (United Church of Christ). "Reactions and Forecasts" were given by Drs. Daniel Migliore and William Lazareth.

At the spring meeting in 1974 in New York a committee composed of Drs. Forell, Wietzke, and Bohlmann presented a paper on the "Lutheran Assessment of the Reformed," and Dr. Arthur C. Cochrane gave a paper on "Descriptive Assessment of the 'Consensus and Remaining Differences' " with responses by Drs. John Leith and Roger Hazleton.

3. The Leuenberg Agreement of 1973, which had been drawn up by representatives of Lutheran, Reformed, and United churches in Europe, has been sent to some ninety churches. "Full pulpit and altar fellowship" will be formally created among the churches signing. It is possible that a formal agreement among our churches in America might have been achieved if our group had recommended that Leuenberg be sent to them to be signed. But for a number of reasons this option was rejected: (a) Leuenberg was criticized by some because of its alleged ambiguities and compromises. (b) Others felt that it is inadequate for our pluralistic society. It does not take account of the sociological factors which have shaped our churches in America: culture, ethos, class, secularization, the protean character of modern existence, etc. An assessment of differences and common understanding of our Christian faith needs to take account of our peculiar and specific history in North America. It is for this reason that a document like the Leuenberg Agreement did not seem to be of particular help to the American situation. (c) Still others felt that the basis of church fellowship cannot be in the settlement of sixteenth-century disputes about the Lord's Supper but in a common confessing of Jesus Christ in the face of contemporary issues facing our churches in America.

We attempted to express our unity in terms other than Leuenberg but were unsuccessful. In gratitude we recognize that we have learned much from one another; in penitence we acknowledge our common need to be open to the work of the Spirit in a fresh hearing of God's word, which alone can create genuine church fellowship in what is proclaimed in our pulpits, is celebrated around the Lord's Table, and is demonstrated in our witness and service.

## II

1. When the official positions of the participating churches with respect to pulpit and altar (table) fellowship were studied, it was found that there has existed and still exists a consensus among Lutheran and Reformed churches concerning the following *doctrinal* points: the Lord's Supper is (1) a sacrament; (2) a means of grace, in which (3) the true (proper) body and blood of Jesus Christ are present and are eaten and drunk. Disagreement remains between Lutheran and Reformed churches, and even among Reformed churches, concerning the *mode* of Christ's presence.

Our discussions have revealed that one of the significant points of remaining differences is a different view in understanding what is meant by "pulpit and altar fellowship." We have discovered that Lutherans tend to give much more weight and significance to the concept "pulpit and altar fellowship" than do the Reformed. There is a variety of understandings that prevails among the churches in the Reformed tradition but overall amongst them there seems to be less packed into the meaning of this concept. It became apparent in this round of conversations that a great deal more attention was given to the question of "altar fellowship" than to any other dimension of relationship between the churches engaged in these conversations.

2. When the *practice* of the participating churches in regard to the Lord's Supper was reviewed, it was observed that most of the Reformed churches have for a long time taught and practiced Communion open to all Christians and recognized the ordination of ministers of other churches. A difference became apparent between The Lutheran Church—Missouri Synod on the one hand, and The American Lutheran Church and the Lutheran Church in America on the other. The Missouri Synod refrains for doctrinal reasons from pulpit and altar fellowship with other church bodies.[4] Although in The American Lutheran Church and the Lutheran Church in America the practice varies in individual congregations, they have in fact been practicing pulpit and altar fellowship. They do not practice "close" Communion, nor do they adhere to a rule of Lutheran pulpits for Lutheran preachers alone, but function under the rubric of "selective fellowship" on these matters.

3. We observed that while The American Lutheran Church and the Lutheran Church in America and the Reformed churches adhere to the *doctrine* of the Lord's Supper expressed in their respective Confessions of faith, in *practice* they are saying that the confessional differences concerning the *mode* of Christ's presence ought not to be re-

garded as obstacles to pulpit and altar fellowship. The differences may involve error, but they do not amount to heresy and therefore to a denial of Jesus Christ as the one Lord and Savior of men. These churches practice a measure of pulpit and altar fellowship without formal agreement, and they have done so on the basis of their respective Confessions of faith.

4. In drawing this report to a close, we would again call attention to the fact that we were asked "to assess the consensus and remaining differences in the theology of the participating churches as they bear upon the teaching of the Gospel in the current situation." In fact, most of our time and energy was spent upon what pulpit and altar fellowship is actual and possible among us *on the basis of our respective traditions*. Our inability to make theological headway may well be related to our concentration on our ecclesiastical traditions instead of a fresh and serious study of Scripture in the current situation.

## III
## RECOMMENDATIONS

In view of our assessment of "the consensus and remaining differences in the theology and life of the participating churches," we recommend to the presidents of the church bodies participating in the Lutheran Council in the U.S.A., and to the North American Area of the World Alliance of Reformed Churches (Presbyterian and Congregational) the following:

1. That this present series of Lutheran-Reformed conversations be considered terminated;

2. That our churches be urged to approach each other, at every level of life, through a fresh hearing of the gospel declared in Holy Scripture, as well as in terms of their confessional and ecclesiastical traditions;

3. That if formal declarations of altar fellowship are desired, this question be dealt with on a church body to church body basis;

4. That in view of appalling needs in the world drawing us to speak and act concretely concerning hunger, oppression, poverty, and all other forms of human misery, our respective churches be urged to recognize and proclaim, in repentance and hope, the judgment and promise of the word of God in our contemporary situation;

5. That in view of the teaching of Scripture and the brokenness of society, we reaffirm our belief in the unity of the church, and express our fervent prayer and hope that the Holy Spirit will lead the whole body of Christ to repentance and renewal.

## PARTICIPANTS

The Report was adopted without dissenting vote* by the dialogue participants at the sixth and final session in Princeton, New Jersey, 27 September 1974. Designated as representatives of their traditions to this series of conversations were:

### Lutheran

Dr. William H. Weiblen, Dubuque, Iowa—The American Lutheran Church

Dr. Walter R. Wietzke, Minneapolis, Minnesota—The American Lutheran Church

Dr. James H. Burtness, St. Paul, Minnesota—The American Lutheran Church (alternate)

Dr. George W. Forell, Iowa City, Iowa—Lutheran Church in America

Dr. William H. Lazareth, Philadelphia, Pennsylvania—Lutheran Church in America

Dr. Arnold E. Carlson, Columbia, South Carolina—Lutheran Church in America (alternate)

Dr. Ralph A. Bohlmann, St. Louis, Missouri—The Lutheran Church—Missouri Synod

Dr. Howard W. Tepker, Springfield, Illinois—The Lutheran Church—Missouri Synod

Dr. Eugene F. Klug, Springfield, Illinois—The Lutheran Church—Missouri Synod (alternate)

Dr. Paul D. Opsahl, New York, New York—Executive Director, Division of Theological Studies, Lutheran Council in the U.S.A. (consultant)

### Reformed

Dr. John H. Leith, Richmond, Virginia—Presbyterian Church in the United States

Dr. Daniel L. Migliore, Princeton, New Jersey—United Presbyterian Church in the U.S.A.

Dr. Thomas D. Parker, Chicago, Illinois—United Presbyterian Church in the U.S.A.

Dr. Arthur C. Cochrane, Pittsburgh, Pennsylvania—United Presbyterian Church in the U.S.A. (alternate)

*Dr. Klug abstained and announced that the other two representatives of The Lutheran Church—Missouri Synod, who were not present at the final session, would also like their abstentions recorded.

Dr. Henry Stob, Grand Rapids, Michigan—Christian Reformed Church

Dr. M. Eugene Osterhaven, Holland, Michigan—Reformed Church in America

Dr. Roger Hazleton, Newton Center, Massachusetts—United Church of Christ

Dr. Robert S. Paul, Pittsburgh, Pennsylvania—United Church of Christ (alternate)

Dr. James I. McCord, Princeton, New Jersey—Secretary, North American Area of the World Alliance of Reformed Churches (Presbyterian and Congregational) (consultant)

NOTES

1. Paul C. Empie and James I. McCord, eds. (Minneapolis: Augsburg Publishing House, 1966).

2. Ibid., p. 191.

3. Two church body actions should, however, be noted. The American Lutheran Church, at its 1966 convention, referred the report of this dialogue series to its Committee on Inter-church Relations. The Lutheran Church—Missouri Synod, at its 1967 convention, voiced appreciation that the conversations had proved fruitful, had manifested a measure of agreement upon the topics discussed, and had frankly recognized and discussed remaining differences. It requested its Commission on Theology and Church Relations, in cooperation with other Lutherans, to take whatever steps would be necessary for participation in further discussion on national and local levels.

4. Except, in North America, for The American Lutheran Church.

APPENDIX 3

# LEUENBERG AGREEMENT*

An Agreement, or Statement of Concord, between the Reformation churches of Europe was adopted by the Preparatory Assembly in completed form on March 16, 1973, in the Swiss conference center of Leuenberg. Intended to foster fellowship between the "Lutheran and Reformed churches in Europe along with the Union churches that grew out of them, and the related pre-Reformation churches, the Waldensian Church and the Church of the Czech Brethren" in terms of mutual recognition, the Leuenberg Agreement, as it has come to be called, has been transmitted to all involved European churches as well as to churches in other parts of the world.

Over the signatures of Dr. André Appel (Lutheran World Federation), Dr. Edmond Perret (World Alliance of Reformed Churches), and Dr. Lukas Vischer (Faith and Order Secretariat, World Council of Churches), a covering letter (March 30, 1973) was sent to the churches participating in the Preparatory Assembly. Strongly supporting the request of the two Assembly chairmen, Professor Max Geiger (Reformed) and Professor Marc Lienhard (Lutheran), the three staff officials expressed the conviction that "all further work must be undertaken in the closest possible contact with the churches themselves."

That the Leuenberg Agreement carries its message to churches in Asia, Africa, Australasia, and the Americas is readily evident. *Lutheran World* here brings two documents: under A. instructions "To the Churches Participating in the Drafting of the Agreement" as to the next steps; and under B. the revised and received text of the Agreement.

## A. TO THE CHURCHES PARTICIPATING IN THE DRAFTING OF THE AGREEMENT

On behalf of the "Preparatory Assembly for the Drafting of an Agreement between the Reformation Churches in Europe," and in accordance with its decision, we are sending you herewith the final text of the Agreement between the Reformation churches in Europe as revised

*Lutheran World* 20 (1973): 347–53.

at the Preparatory Assembly's second meeting from March 12–16, 1973, with the request that your church should take the necessary steps to reach a decision on the acceptance of the Agreement.

1. The European churches having noted the Schauenburg Theses (1967) and being largely in agreement with them, at their express wish and with their direct participation the so-called "Leuenberg Conversations" were held (1969–1970). The main theme of these conversations was the question of church fellowship. The churches' official representatives at these conversations recommended that work be begun on drafting an Agreement which could form the basis for achieving church fellowship. Having noted and approved this recommendation, the churches appointed their delegates for the drafting of the text of an Agreement. Meeting in Leuenberg from September 19–24, 1971, the official delegates of the churches produced the draft of an Agreement between the Reformation churches of Europe.

2. In September, 1971, the Preparatory Assembly set up a Continuation Committee which made preparations for the second meeting of the Preparatory Assembly in March, 1973. In accordance with its mandate, the Continuation Committee held several meetings to consider the replies received from the churches, and proposed a revised version of the text of the Agreement. In respect of the requests of a few churches, the Continuation Committee itself was unable to establish a final text of the Agreement. At its second meeting, the Preparatory Assembly had before it a report from the Continuation Committee as well as the Committee's written proposals for changes in the text of the Agreement. It also received and considered a synopsis of the replies from the churches, together with a number of comments from church groups and individuals. Up to that time, replies had been received from 63 churches, and a further 9 churches were able to inform the Assembly about their preliminary discussions by means of detailed documents, even although their final answers were still not completed.

3. It was with thankfulness and joy that the Preparatory Assembly discovered that the churches represented in it were practically unanimous in their resolve to continue to seek church fellowship between the Reformation churches of Europe on the basis of an agreement. This was all the more remarkable because many of the churches, in determining their official response, had not only taken into account the views of professional theologians and university faculties but had also to a large extent drawn their ordained ministers and congregations into the process of reaching a common mind.

4. In the light of its study of the comments received, the Preparatory Assembly decided to base all its further work and decisions on

this unanimity of the churches in approving the choice of an Agreement as the goal and the method to be pursued. It became convinced that, once the text had been revised, what could be done had been done, and that its work had therefore come to its conclusion. It believes that the matter would not be furthered substantially were the churches invited to comment again, and it therefore now requests the participant churches to accept the Agreement.

5. Important changes suggested have been incorporated in this revised text, and as far as possible a number of basic questions have been clarified.

Wherever possible, the language of the draft text has been improved in response to the criticisms expressed in some of the replies. It should, of course, be borne in mind that the doctrinal differences, which it was the purpose of the Agreement to overcome, are formulated in the characteristic language of the confessions or traditions. In dealing with these verbal formulations of doctrine, therefore, it was necessary to employ a corresponding style. The Preparatory Assembly was fully aware that the task of finding a contemporary language still confronts the churches, and must be tackled in the continuing doctrinal discussions.

In revising the text, care was taken not to add any new propositions. The Agreement does not need to treat every subject dealt with in the confessions and traditions of the individual churches. But it was also essential not to tighten and abbreviate the text to the detriment of the common understanding of the gospel which is required as the basis of the church fellowship into which the churches are to enter. After full discussion the Preparatory Assembly decided that a short form of declaration, giving just a brief account of the consensus which exists between the churches, would not suffice for an affirmation of church fellowship.

*6. The Procedure for the Reception*

a) The text of the Agreement between the Reformation churches of Europe adopted by the second Preparatory Assembly is attested by the signatures of the four chairmen of the Preparatory Assembly, namely, Dr. Max Geiger of Basle, Dr. Leonhard Goppelt of Munich, Dr. Horst Lahr of Potsdam, and Dr. Marc Lienhard of Strasbourg. The signed document is deposited with the World Council of Churches, and copies of it with the Lutheran World Federation and the World Alliance of Reformed Churches.

b) The participant churches are invited to indicate their assent in writing by September 30, 1974

c) The following declaration should be included in the written assent: "The . . . (name of the church) . . . assents to the version of the Agreement between the Reformation churches of Europe (the Leuenberg Agreement) adopted on March 16, 1973."
d) Declarations of assent should be sent to the World Council of Churches (Faith and Order Commission, 150 route de Ferney, 1211 Geneva 20, Switzerland) where they will be deposited. Participant churches will be informed of each declaration of assent received by the World Council of Churches.
e) Church fellowship in the sense indicated in the Agreement will come into effect on October 1, 1974, between those churches whose declaration of assent has then been received by the World Council of Churches.
f) Churches whose declaration of assent reaches the World Council of Churches after September 30, 1974, will be participants in church fellowship in the sense indicated in the Agreement from the date on which their declaration is received.

7. The Preparatory Assembly made the following proposals concerning the achievement of church fellowship.

a) The participant churches are asked to send in suggestions and requests concerning the practical realization of church fellowship, together with subjects for the proposed continuing doctrinal conversations.
b) If possible, these doctrinal conversations should be initiated still in 1974. Invitations to participate in them will be sent even to those churches which have not yet been able to reach a decision to assent to the Agreement by the time the doctrinal discussions are resumed. The Continuation Committee will discuss detailed arrangements with the Lutheran World Federation and the World Alliance of Reformed Churches.
c) The Preparatory Assembly came to the opinion that the calling of a "General Assembly" as envisaged in earlier letters can for the present be disregarded. This does not exclude the possibility of calling a General Assembly at a date to be specified later, if the participant churches consider this desirable. It could, for example, take place in conjunction with the beginning of the continuing doctrinal discussions.

8. The Continuation Committee appointed by the Preparatory Assembly consists of the following members: Professor Dr. Andreas Aarflot (Professor Dr. Holsten Faberberg); Bishop Helge Brattgård (Professor Dr. Fredric Cleve); The Rev. Martin H. Cressey (The Rev. Professor Allan D. Galloway); Professor Dr. Wilhelm Dantine (Prelate

Dr. Albrecht Hege); Bishop Dr. Emerich Varga (Pastor Johan A. Dvoracek); Professor Dr. Max Geiger (Professor Dr. Louis Rumpf); Professor Dr. Leonhard Goppelt (Bishop Dr. Friedrich Hübner); Oberkirchenrat (retired) Dr. Karl Herberg (Prelate Dr. Hans Bornhäuser); Pastor Attila Kovach (Pastor G. Gyula Röhrig); General Superintendent Dr. Horst Lahr (Oberkirchenrat Dr. Werner Tannert); Professor Dr. Marc Lienhard (Pastor Alain Blancy); Oberkirchenrat Olav Lingner (Oberkirchenrat Dr. Werner Hofmann); Professor Dr. Wenzel Lohff (Dr. Hans Martin Müller); Dr. Remko J. Mooi (Professor Dr. Daniel Vidal); Dr. Paolo Ricca; President Hugo Schnell (Oberkirchenrat Hermann Greifenstein); Praeses Professor Dr. Joachim Staedtke (Landessuperintendent Dr. Gerhard Nordholt).

It is the responsibility of the Continuation Committee to carry out the tasks mentioned in paragraphs 6 and 7.

Signed on behalf of the Preparatory Assembly.

Professor Dr. Max Geiger, *Chairman*

Professor Dr. Marc Lienhard, *Chairman*

## B. AGREEMENT BETWEEN REFORMATION CHURCHES IN EUROPE (LEUENBERG AGREEMENT)

(1) On the basis of their doctrinal discussions, the churches assenting to this Agreement—namely, Lutheran and Reformed churches in Europe along with the Union churches which grew out of them, and the related pre-Reformation churches, the Waldensian Church and the Church of the Czech Brethren—affirm together the common understanding of the gospel elaborated below. This common understanding of the gospel enables them to declare and to realize church fellowship. Thankful that they have been led closer together, they confess at the same time that guilt and suffering have also accompanied and still accompany the struggle for truth and unity in the church.

(2) The church is founded upon Jesus Christ alone. It is he who gathers the church and sends it forth, by the bestowal of his salvation in preaching and the sacraments. In the view of the Reformation, it follows that agreement in the right teaching of the gosepl, and in the right administration of the sacraments, is the necessary and sufficient prerequisite for the true unity of the church. It is from these Reformation criteria that the participating churches derive their view of church fellowship as set out below.

## I. The Road to Fellowship

(3) Faced with real differences in style of theological thinking and church practice, the fathers of the Reformation, despite much that they had in common, did not see themselves in a position, on grounds of faith and conscience, to avoid divisions. In this Agreement the participating churches acknowledge that their relationship to one another has changed since the time of the Reformation.

### 1. *Common Aspects at the Outset of the Reformation*

(4) With the advantage of historical distance, it is easier today to discern the common elements in the witness of the churches of the Reformation, in spite of the differences between them: "Their starting point was a new experience of the power of the gospel to liberate and assure. In standing up for the truth which they saw, the Reformers found themselves drawn together in opposition to the church traditions of that time. They were, therefore, at one in confessing that the church's life and doctrine are to be gauged by the original and pure testimony to the gospel in Scripture. They were at one in bearing witness to God's free and unconditional grace in the life, death, and resurrection of Jesus Christ for all those who believe this promise. They were at one in confessing that the practice and form of the church should be determined only by the commission to deliver this testimony to the world, and that the word of God remains sovereign over every human ordering of the Christian community. In so doing, they were at one with the whole of Christendom in receiving and renewing the confession of the triune God and the God-manhood of Jesus Christ as expressed in the ancient creeds of the church.

### 2. *Changed Elements in the Contemporary Situation*

(5) In the course of 400 years of history, the churches of the Reformation have been led to new and similar ways of thinking and living: by theological wrestling with the questions of modern times, by advances in biblical research, by the movements of church renewal, and by the rediscovery of the ecumenical horizon. These developments certainly have also brought with them new differences cutting right across the confessions. But, time and again, there has also been an experience of brotherly fellowship, particularly in times of common suffering. The result of all these factors was a new concern on the part of the churches, especially since the revival movement, to achieve a contemporary expression both of the biblical witness and of the Reformation

confessions of faith. In the process they have learned to distinguish between the fundamental witness of the Reformation confessions of faith and their historically-conditioned thought forms. Because these confessions of faith bear witness to the gospel as the living word of God in Jesus Christ, far from barring the way to continued responsible testimony to the Word, they open up this way with a summons to follow it in the freedom of faith.

## II. The Common Understanding of the Gospel

(6) In what follows, the participating churches describe their common understanding of the gospel insofar as this is required for establishing church fellowship between them.

### *1. The Message of Justification as the Message of the Free Grace of God*

(7) The gospel is the message of Jesus Christ, the salvation of the world, in fulfilment of the promise given to the people of the Old Covenant.

(8) a) The true understanding of the gospel was expressed by the fathers of the Reformation in the doctrine of justification.

(9) b) In this message, Jesus Christ is acknowledged as the one in whom God became man and bound himself to man; as the crucified and risen one who took God's judgment upon himself and, in so doing, demonstrated God's love to sinners; and as the coming one who, as Judge and Savior, leads the world to its consummation.

(10) c) Through his word, God by his Holy Spirit calls all men to repent and believe, and assures the believing sinner of his righteousness in Jesus Christ. Whoever puts his trust in the gospel is justified in God's sight for the sake of Jesus Christ, and set free from the accusation of the law. In daily repentance and renewal, he lives within the fellowship in praise of God and in service to others, in the assurance that God will bring his kingdom in all its fulness. In this way, God creates new life, and plants in the midst of the world the seed of a new humanity.

(11) d) This message sets Christians free for responsible service in the world and makes them ready to suffer in this service. They know that God's will, as demand and succour, embraces the whole world. They stand up for temporal justice and peace between individuals and nations. To do this they have to join with others in seeking rational and appropriate criteria, and play their part in applying these criteria. They do so in the confidence that God sustains the world and as those who are accountable to him.

(12) e) In this understanding of the gospel, we take our stand on the basis of the ancient creeds of the church, and reaffirm the common conviction of the Reformation confessions that the unique mediation of Jesus Christ in salvation is the heart of the Scriptures, and that the message of justification as the message of God's free grace is the measure of all the church's preaching.

### 2. *Preaching, Baptism, and the Lord's Supper*

(13) The fundamental witness to the gospel is the testimony of the apostles and prophets in the Holy Scriptures of the Old and New Testaments. It is the task of the church to spread this gospel by the spoken word in preaching, by individual counselling, and by baptism and the Lord's Supper. In preaching, baptism, and the Lord's Supper, Jesus Christ is present through the Holy Spirit. Justification in Christ is thus imparted to men, and in this way the Lord gathers his people. In doing so he employs various forms of ministry and service, as well as the witness of all those belonging to his people.

#### a) Baptism

(14) Baptism is administered in the name of the Father and of the Son and of the Holy Spirit with water. In baptism, Jesus Christ irrevocably receives man, fallen prey to sin and death, into his fellowship of salvation so that he may become a new creature. In the power of his Holy Spirit, he calls him into his community and to a new life of faith, to daily repentance, and to discipleship.

#### b) The Lord's Supper

(15) In the Lord's Supper the risen Christ imparts himself in his body and blood, given up for all, through his word of promise with bread and wine. He thereby grants us forgiveness of sins, and sets us free for a new life of faith. He enables us to experience anew that we are members of his body. He strengthens us for service to all men.

(16) When we celebrate the Lord's Supper we proclaim the death of Christ through which God has reconciled the world with himself. We proclaim the presence of the risen Lord in our midst. Rejoicing that the Lord has come to us, we await his future coming in glory.

## III. Accord in Respect of the Doctrinal Condemnations of the Reformation Era

(17) The differences which from the time of the Reformation onwards have made church fellowship between Lutheran and Reformed

churches impossible, and have led them to pronounce mutual condemnations, relate to the doctrine of the Lord's Supper, christology, and the doctrine of predestination. We take the decisions of the Reformation fathers seriously, but are today able to agree on the following statements in respect of these condemnations:

*1. The Lord's Supper*

(18) In the Lord's Supper the risen Jesus Christ imparts himself in his body and blood, given up for all, through his word of promise with bread and wine. He thus gives himself unreservedly to all who receive the bread and wine; faith receives the Lord's Supper for salvation, unfaith for judgment.

(19) We cannot separate communion with Jesus Christ in his body and blood from the act of eating and drinking. To be concerned about the manner of Christ's presence in the Lord's Supper in abstraction from this act is to run the risk of obscuring the meaning of the Lord's Supper.

(20) Where such a consensus exists between the churches, the condemnations pronounced by the Reformation confessions are inapplicable to the doctrinal position of these churches.

*2. Christology*

(21) In the true man Jesus Christ, the eternal Son, and so God himself, has bestowed himself upon lost mankind for its salvation. In the word of the promise and in the sacraments, the Holy Spirit, and so God himself, makes the crucified and risen Jesus present to us.

(22) Believing in this self-bestowal of God in his Son, the task facing us, in view of the historically-conditioned character of traditional thought forms, is to give renewed and effective expression to the special insights of the Reformed tradition, with its concern to maintain unimpaired the divinity and humanity of Jesus, and to those of the Lutheran tradition, with its concern to maintain the unity of Jesus as a person.

(23) In these circumstances, it is impossible for us to reaffirm the former condemnations today

*3. Predestination*

(24) In the gospel we have the promise of God's unconditional acceptance of sinful man. Whoever puts his trust in the gospel can know that he is saved, and praise God for his election. For this reason we can speak of election only with respect to the call to salvation in Christ.

(25) Faith knows by experience that the message of salvation is not

accepted by all; yet it respects the mystery of God's dealings with men. It bears witness to the seriousness of human decisions, and at the same time to the reality of God's universal purpose of salvation. The witness of the Scriptures to Christ forbids us to suppose that God has uttered an eternal decree for the final condemnation of specific individuals or of a particular people.

(26) When such a consensus exists between churches, the condemnations pronounced by the Reformation confessions of faith are inapplicable to the doctrinal position of these churches.

*4. Conclusions*

(27) Wherever these statements are accepted, the condemnations of the Reformation confessions in respect of the Lord's Supper, christology, and predestination are inapplicable to the doctrinal position. This does not mean that the condemnations pronounced by the Reformation fathers are irrelevant; but they are no longer an obstacle to church fellowship.

(28) There remain considerable differences between our churches in forms of worship, types of spirituality, and church order. These differences are often more deeply felt in the congregations than the traditional doctrinal differences. Nevertheless, in fidelity to the New Testament and Reformation criteria for church fellowship, we cannot discern in these differences any factors which should divide the church.

## IV. The Declaration and Realization of Church Fellowship

(29) In the sense intended in this Agreement, church fellowship means that, on the basis of the consensus they have reached in their understanding of the gospel, churches with different confessional positions accord each other fellowship in word and sacrament, and strive for the fullest possible cooperation in witness and service to the world.

*1. Declaration of Church Fellowship*

(30) In assenting to this Agreement the churches, in loyalty to the confessions of faith which bind them, or with due respect for their traditions, declare:

(31) a) that they are one in understanding the gospel as set out in Parts II and III;

(32) b) that, in accordance with what is said in Part III, the doctrinal condemnations expressed in the confessional documents no longer apply to the contemporary doctrinal position of the assenting churches;

(33) c) that they accord each other table and pulpit fellowship; this includes the mutual recognition of ordination and the freedom to provide for intercelebration.

(34) With these statements, church fellowship is declared. The divisions which have barred the way to this fellowship since the 16th century are removed. The participating churches are convinced that they have been put together in the one church of Jesus Christ, and that the Lord liberates them for, and lays upon them the obligation of, common service.

2. *Realizing Church Fellowship*

(35) It is in the life of the churches and congregations that church fellowship becomes a reality. Believing in the unifying power of the Holy Spirit, they bear their witness and perform their service together, and strive to deepen and strengthen the fellowship they have found together.

a) Witness and Service

(36) The preaching of the churches gains credibility in the world when they are at one in their witness to the gospel. The gospel liberates and binds together the churches to render common service. Being the service of love, it turns to man in his distress and seeks to remove the causes of that distress. The struggle for justice and peace in the world increasingly demands of the churches the acceptance of a common responsibility.

b) The Continuing Theological Task

(37) The Agreement leaves intact the binding force of the confessions within the participating churches. It is not to be regarded as a new confession of faith. It sets forth a consensus reached about central matters; one which makes church fellowship possible between churches of different confessional positions. In accordance with this consensus, the participating churches will seek to establish a common witness and service, and pledge themselves to their common doctrinal discussions.

(38) The common understanding of the gospel on which church fellowship is based must be further deepened, tested in the light of the witness of Holy Scripture, and continually made relevant in the contemporary scene.

(39) The churches have the task of studying further these differences of doctrine which, while they do not have divisive force, still persist within and between the participating churches. These include: her-

meneutical questions concerning the understanding of Scripture, confession of faith, and church; the relation between law and gospel; baptismal practice; ministry and ordination; the "two kingdom" doctrine, and the doctrine of the sovereignty of Christ; and church and society. At the same time newly emerging problems relating to witness and service, order and practice, have to be considered.

(40) On the basis of their common heritage, the churches of the Reformation must determine their attitude to trends toward theological polarization increasingly in evidence today. To some extent the problems here go beyond the doctrinal differences which were once at the basis of the Lutheran-Reformed controversy.

(41) It will be the task of common theological study to testify to the truth of the gospel and to distinguish it from all distortions.

c) Organizational Consequences

(42) This declaration of church fellowship does not anticipate provisions of church law on particular matters of inter-church relations, or within the churches. The churches will, however, take the Agreement into account considering such provisions.

(43) As a general rule, the affirmation of pulpit and table fellowship and the mutual recognition of ordination do not affect the rules in force in the participating churches for induction to a pastoral charge, the exercise of the pastoral ministry, or the ordering of congregational life.

(44) The question of organic union between particular participating churches can only be decided in the situation in which these churches live. In examining this question the following points should be kept in mind:

(45) Any union detrimental to the lively plurality in styles of preaching, ways of worship, church order, and in diaconal and social action, would contradict the very nature of the church fellowship inaugurated by this declaration. On the other hand, in certain situations, because of the intimate connection between witness and order, the church's service may call for formal legal unification. Where organizational consequences are drawn from this declaration, it should not be at the expense of freedom of decision in minority churches.

d) Ecumenical Aspects

(46) In establishing and realizing church fellowship among themselves, the participating churches do so as part of their responsibility to promote the ecumenical fellowship of all Christian churches.

(47) They regard such a fellowship of churches in the European area as a contribution to this end. They hope that the ending of their pre-

vious separation will influence churches in Europe and elsewhere who are related to them confessionally. They are ready to examine with them the possibilities of wider church fellowship.

(48) This hope applies equally to the relationship between the Lutheran World Federation and the World Alliance of Reformed Churches.

(49) They also hope that the achievement of church fellowship with each other will provide a fresh stimulus to conference and cooperation with churches of other confessions. They affirm their readiness to set their doctrinal discussions within this wider context.

APPENDIX 4

# A STATEMENT ON COMMUNION PRACTICES BY THE AMERICAN LUTHERAN CHURCH— LUTHERAN CHURCH IN AMERICA

Advent 1978

Members, Congregations and Clergy
The American Lutheran Church and
the Lutheran Church in America

Dear Members of The Body of Christ:

The American Lutheran Church and the Lutheran Church in America adopted a common Statement on Communion Practices at their respective 1978 conventions. The statement is one of the fruits of the churches' partnership in life and mission.

As you study this statement, it may be helpful to you to know some of the needs which led our churches to develop a new and common statement. In addition to our commitment to cooperation and common witness, these needs were identified:

—A need to clarify the role of lay persons in the administration of the Sacrament. This was prompted both by the increasing involvement of lay persons as assistants in the public worship and also by questions about lay admininstration to the sick and homebound.

—A need to take a fresh look at the matter of intercommunion. In view of historic Lutheran practice, current congregational practices and the results of interconfessional dialogs make this need imperative.

—A need to rethink the question of admission to Holy Communion. This included incorporating the recommendations of the Joint Commission on Theology and Practice of Confirmation, which both churches adopted in 1970.

—A need to answer questions about the role of confession and absolution in relation to the Sacrament. These questions arise as a result of the gradual movement of congregations toward a more celebrative emphasis in connection with Holy Communion.

There are also a variety of practical questions to which a statement such as this provides answers.

We commend this statement to you for your study and use. Where possible, we hope clergy of our two churches will study it together, using that study as an occasion to reflect upon our common faith, witness, and practice. Additional copies may be secured from the ALC Augsburg Publishing House and the LCA Division for Parish Services. A study book is being prepared for use among parish groups and will be available early in the new year.

We pray that the Lord of the Church will use this statement as one means to enrich our understanding of and appreciation for Holy Communion.

In Christ,

David W. Preus, *President*
The American Lutheran Church

James R. Crumley, Jr., *President*
Lutheran Church in America

# A Statement on Communion Practices

A Statement of The American Lutheran Church and the Lutheran Church in America. The Theological Introduction (Section I) was received and the Recommendations for Practice (Section II) were adopted by the 1978 conventions of the two churches.

## I. THEOLOGICAL INTRODUCTION

### Christ Offered

1. The treasure of the Church is the good news that God was in Christ reconciling the world unto himself. Through his life, death, and resurrection Christ freely offers himself to us through the Word and the Sacraments in the fellowship of faith.

### Images and Concepts

2. Various images and concepts have been used to describe the Sacrament in which Christ gives himself anew to the believing community. Among Christians it has been referred to as the Lord's Supper, the Holy Communion, the Sacrament of the Altar, and the Eucharist. Among Lutherans motifs of remembrance, fellowship, thanksgiving, confession and forgiveness, and celebration have been incorporated. Whatever images and concepts are used the intention and emphasis of the biblical witness and of our tradition has been to assert and affirm God's gift of grace through the body and blood of Christ, "given and shed" for us.

### Means of Grace

3. The Sacrament of Holy Communion is a Means of Grace from God to his people through which the crucified and risen Christ is present and active to forgive, to save, to unite, to give life, to comfort, and to strengthen for the work to which he calls his people in the world. The Lutheran Confessions uphold the reality of Christ's presence in the Sacrament, his body and blood being given "in, with and under" the bread and the wine, in order to affirm by these means his saving work for us.* Luther sums up his understanding of this last will and

*It is the responsibility of our churches to teach clearly this Lutheran doctrine of the Lord's Supper and to witness to it in dealing with other churches. Fulfilling the obligation to the truth in this way makes it possible to express the unity of the Church at the Lord's table with those who affirm the Real Presence of Christ in the Sacrament but who

testament of Christ by saying: "In this Sacrament he offers all the treasure he brought from heaven for us. . . . " (LC V, 66). In response to our Lord's command, "This do in remembrance of me," the promise is spoken and the bread and the wine are given and received in liturgical actions, whereby we "proclaim his death until he comes" (1 Corinthians 11:26).

## God's Promised Gift

4. The meaning and significance of the Holy Communion consists in its character as God's promised gift offered to us and for us. Communion signifies and renews the community given to the world in the death and resurrection of Jesus Christ and in which we participate through Baptism. Because of the saving love of God in Christ conveyed in the Sacrament the language and spirit of the service is one of thanksgiving (*eucharistia*). We remember the mighty acts of God, we receive the gift of the presence of Christ, and look forward in anticipation to the fulfillment of all things in the Kingdom of God. Through the power of the Holy Spirit this remembrance, presence, and anticipation becomes a reality in our lives, and we receive in this meal a foretaste of the things to come.

## Covenant

5. The theme of covenant is important to the biblical understanding of the people of God. It describes an aspect of the relationship between God and his chosen people. God's involvement in human history has had the object of forming out of common and fallen humanity a covenant community of people who are his own. In the fullness of time this covenant was made new through Jesus the Christ and through his Holy Spirit given to the Church. This new covenant (Jeremiah 31:31, ff.), initiated and ratified by Christ's self-offering (Matthew 26:28; Mark 14:24) is now ours, proclaimed in Word and Sacrament in the Church, and witnessed to in the Christian life. Holy Baptism is the means by which one is incorporated into the community of the new covenant. Holy Communion is a means by which this new relationship to God and the Church is nourished and strengthened.

---

use formulations to describe it other than those used in the Lutheran Confessions. Accordingly the Recommendations for Practice provide guidelines for admission of others than Lutherans to the Sacrament and considerations for Lutheran participation in intercommunion. Within these provisions the responsibility for decision about communing is placed upon the communicants. Such practice is consistent with the Large Catechism, V, 2.

**Sacrament**

6. The Lord's Supper is a sacrament, that is, God's gift of Christ's presence and love to us. It is not essentially an act or rite in which we give something to God. However, believers, confronted by the magnitude of God's grace in Jesus Christ, and the promise of forgiveness, life, and salvation, here presented in visible proclamation, respond in faith, obedience, and love. The Holy Spirit arouses faith whereby we turn to and trust in Christ alone. The Holy Spirit also moves those who believe to love other people as Christ himself does. This response is a "living sacrifice" of everything we are and have to God (Romans 12:1), which according to the Lutheran confessions includes "'sacrifices of praise': the proclamation of the Gospel, faith, prayer, thanksgiving, confession, the afflictions of the saints, yes, all the good works of the saints" (AP XXIV, 25). The response must never be confused with the gift. The Holy Communion is a service celebrating reconciliation. It is a Means of Grace by which the common life of God's new community is fostered and sustained and this new people is propelled into the world to engage in the mission which they have been given.

## II. RECOMMENDATIONS FOR PRACTICE

### A. Participants in Holy Communion

*1. Communicants*

Holy Communion is the sacramental meal of the new people of God who are called and incorporated into the body of Christ through baptism. Whenever the sacrament is celebrated it should be open to all such people who are present and ready for admission.

*2. Admission*

Admission to the Sacrament is by invitation of the Lord, presented through the Church to those who are baptized. It is the practice of the Church to admit to Holy Communion those who, in its judgment, are ready to participate. The decision regarding readiness should be informed by the following guidelines, which are consistent with our confessions:

a. That there be a simple trust that the Crucified and Risen Lord is here truly present, giving himself to his people, as his words declare;

b. That there be a basic understanding and appreciation of the gifts God gives through the sacrament;
c. That there be an acceptance of one's place as a communicant in the fellowship of believers; and
d. That there be self-examination in a manner appropriate to the level of maturity and recognition of the need of forgiveness.

There may be special concern for the admission of children. The findings of the Joint Commission on Theology and Practice of Confirmation indicate that readiness to participate normally occurs at age ten or the level of fifth grade, but it may occur earlier or later. The responsibility for deciding when to admit a child is shared by the pastor, the child, the family or sponsoring persons, and the congregation. Thus infant communion is precluded.

### 3. *Preparation for Communion*

Personal preparation should be encouraged as a means of becoming more receptive to God's gifts in Communion. Such preparation does not make one "worthy." "He is truly worthy and well prepared, who believes these words: 'For you' and 'for the forgiveness of sins' " (SC V1, 10). Helpful forms of preparation may include self-examination and prayer, setting things right with one's estranged brothers and sisters, meditating on the appointed Scripture readings, etc. Meditation on one's place in the Body of Christ and thus in the Church's mission is also helpful preparation.

### 4. *Confession*

Corporate confession with its proclamation of forgiveness has great value and is a normal preparation for the celebration of Holy Communion. Opportunity for private confession and absolution should be provided in every parish. Both private and corporate confession and absolution may be used independently of the Communion service.

### 5. *The Presiding Minister*

It is the gathered people of God who celebrate the Sacrament. But in accordance with the Lutheran Confessions and traditional church practice, the pastor, as the one duly called and ordained for the Ministry of Word and Sacrament, shall preside at the Holy Communion (AC XIV). Only one minister shall preside over the entire celebration. Other clergy present may fill assisting roles.

Lay persons may be authorized by the president of the church or of the appropriate synod/district to preside in those situations where an ordained person is not available for an extended period of time.

Properly trained lay persons may assist in the distribution when approved by the worshiping community. The appropriate liturgical role for seminarians at celebrations of Holy Communion is to serve as assisting ministers. Ordained persons without call may preside at Communion services according to the regulations of the church body.

6. *Authorization*

Authorization for all celebrations of Communion in a parish setting where there is a called minister of Word and Sacrament is the responsibility of the pastor in consultation with the church council.

In established centers of the church, e.g., seminaries, colleges, retreat centers, charitable institutions, and administrative centers, authorization for the celebration of Holy Communion shall be given either for a limited or an unlimited period by the president of the church or, where only one synod/district is concerned, by the president of that synod/district.

In institutions not formally associated with the church, e.g., hospitals, retirement homes, colleges/universities, military bases, where there is a called pastor or chaplain, authorization for the celebration of Holy Communion rests with the pastor in consultation with the calling-sending agency/board of the church.

7. *Intercommunion*

The practice of intercommunion among Lutherans at home and abroad is encouraged.

Participation as a visitor in non-Lutheran congregations, proper because of the universal nature of the Church, places one in the role of guest. As a visitor one should respect the prevailing practice of hospitality. On such occasions and at ecumenical gatherings, in parish and nonparish settings, both pastoral and lay participation as communicants is a matter of personal judgment.

Such judgment should be informed by the following considerations:

a. That the participants be baptized Christians;
b. That the Real Presence of Christ in the Sacrament be publicly affirmed;
c. That the Sacrament be celebrated as a Means of Grace;
d. That the Words of Institution be proclaimed; and
e. That the elements associated with our Lord's institution be used.

For Lutheran clergy to be involved as presiding or assisting ministers in the celebration of Holy Communion in other churches, a reciprocal relationship between the congregations and clergy involved should prevail.

## B. Occasions for Communion

### *1. Places of Celebration*

Holy Communion is normally celebrated in the place where the congregation, i.e., the assembly of believers, meets for worship. Occasionally the church council, in response to specific requests, may authorize the pastor to preside at services where only a portion of the congregation is invited, e.g., meetings in homes or retreat settings. (cf. IIA, 5, par. 1)

Sick and homebound members should be included in the Communion of the congregation. One way to provide such participation is through a visit during which the pastor administers the Communion to those who are present. Another way is by sending pastors or trained and designated lay members out from the corporate worship to the sick and the homebound. Elements from the congregation's celebration may be used. A rite used in these cases shall include the Words of Institution and the Lord's Prayer. The second method of ministering to the sick and homebound members is intended neither to suggest a concept of "reserved elements" nor depart from the traditional role of the pastor (A–5, "Presiding Minister") but is intended to be seen as an extension of the congregation's service of Holy Communion. It provides these persons an opportunity to be included in the worship of the congregation and to receive the benefits of the Sacrament.

Persons isolated from normal congregational life because of residency in institutions or in the military should regularly be offered the opportunity to receive the Sacrament. Where there are institutional or military chaplains they shall provide such opportunity. Where there are no chaplains local pastors should meet this need. In such situations a statement of a Lutheran understanding of the Lord's Supper shall be made with an invitation to baptized Christians who desire to participate.

### *2. Frequency of Celebration*

The earliest Lutheran practice provides an appropriate goal for the frequency of celebration of the full service of Word and Sacrament. "In our churches Mass is celebrated every Sunday and on other festivals when the Sacrament is offered to those who wish for it after they have been examined and absolved" (AP XXIV, 1).

Congregations are encouraged to move toward this goal because the complete service of Holy Communion embodies the fullness of the Means of Grace, because it provides an excellent focus for the whole Christian life and mission, and because it witnesses to our confessional and ecumenical heritage. Our parishes are encouraged to provide for weekday celebrations for the increasing number of Christians whose schedules make Sunday Communion difficult.

Frequency of celebration and frequency of reception should not be confused. The church must make the sacrament available for all who desire it. The decision whether or not to avail one's self of this means of grace is a personal matter. Yet it is the hope of the church that increasing numbers of its people will make the sacrament a normal, rather than an occasional part of their lives.

Consistent pastoral encouragement and instruction relating to Holy Communion should be given in the congregations pointing up Christ's command, his promise, and our deep need (1 Corinthians 11:24–25; LC V, 45–84).

### 3. *The Fullness of the Service*

The Communion Service should normally be celebrated according to the service books provided by the church. When a shorter service is needed the unity of Word and Sacrament should be carefully maintained. In no case should Communion be appended to an Office such as Matins or Vespers. The practice of dismissing a part of the congregation after the Ante-Communion is discouraged.

## C. The Elements of Communion

### 1. *The Use of Bread and Wine*

Lutherans have been concerned to follow the biblical example established in the institution of the Lord's Supper and thus to use the elements of bread and wine.

### 2. *Setting Apart the Elements*

In setting apart the elements for Holy Communion, the Lutheran tradition has focused upon the proclamation of the Words of Institution. A prayer of thanksgiving which includes the Words of Institution, though not a normative practice within the Lutheran tradition, has been the dominant Christian usage and has been included in our orders of worship.

Only enough bread and wine should be brought to the altar to serve the congregation. Should the supply need to be replenished, it is not necessary to repeat the Words of Institution.

Bread and wine remaining on the altar after all have communed may be kept for future use, except that wine remaining in a common cup should not be kept.

### 3. *Distribution and Reception of the Elements*

The manner of distribution and the posture of the communicants may be determined by the worshiping community. A precise manner should not be an issue. What is important is that practices provide the image of unity, reflecting the unity God has given.

Continuous communion of the whole congregation underscores the aspects of fellowship and unity. Standing or kneeling are both acceptable postures for reception. Pastors will find ways to facilitate the communion of the infirm. Whatever the form of distribution of the elements, the words "for you" should be included in those spoken to each communicant. The *one* loaf and the *one* cup evoke the image of the unity of the many who participate in the broken loaf and the cup *of blessing* (I Corinthians 10:16–17). Where individual glasses are used they may be held in the hands of the communicants and be filled from a chalice fitted with a pouring lip or filled in advance of the service.

In keeping with the custom of the early Church the practice of placing the bread in the communicant's hand rather than the mouth is encouraged.

The use of only one element is acceptable where there are special difficulties. Under certain circumstances the practice of intinction, i.e., the dipping of the bread into the wine, may be followed. Ordinarily, however, our people will find the separate reception of both elements to be a more adequate expression of eating and drinking in the sacramental meal. It is appropriate within the Lutheran tradition that the presiding minister commune himself/herself or receive the Sacrament from an assistant.

Reception of the elements does not complete the service. It is therefore appropriate that all communicants remain until the concluding benediction.

# CONSTITUTIONAL DIRECTIVES ON COMMUNION PRACTICE IN THE REFORMED CHURCH IN AMERICA AND THE PRESBYTERIAN CHURCH (U.S.A.)

## THE BOOK OF CHURCH ORDER*

Chapter 1, The Government
The Reformed Church in America

Part I, Article 2, Sec. 6

c. The sacrament of the Lord's Supper shall be administered, if possible, at least once every three months in every church. "The Office for the Administration of the Lord's Supper" shall be read. Whenever the supper is served, all communicant members of the church present are to be invited to participate.
d. The hymns used in public worship shall be in harmony with the Standards of the Reformed Church in America.
e. The consistory of a church shall not invite or permit ministers of other denominations whose character and standard are not known to preach for them. Before such persons may be engaged for that purpose, they shall furnish evidence of recent date, in writing, of their good ministerial standing and of their authorization to preach the Word. The consistory shall then determine whether an invitation to preach should be issued.
f. The points of doctrine contained in the Heidelberg Catechism shall be explained by the minister at regular services of worship on the Lord's Day, so that the exposition of them is completed within a period of four years.

Sec. 7

The consistory shall make provision for the private administration of the sacraments in instances of sickness or other emergency. At least one elder shall be present with the minister on such occasions. At least one other elder shall accompany an elder administering the sacraments privately.

*(New York: Reformed Church Press, 1982 ed.), pp. 16–17.

## THE CONSTITUTION OF THE PRESBYTERIAN CHURCH (U.S.A.)**

Part II, *Book of Order*

### The Lord's Supper

*Many Meanings*

Whereas in the Sacrament of Baptism, God receives persons once for all into the household of faith, in the Sacrament of the Lord's Supper, God offers them continued spiritual nourishment and sustains them in the communion of the body of Christ. Christians have differing names for this holy meal, but all of these signify the one Sacrament. It is sometimes called the Lord's Supper, recalling its institution by Christ when the apostles were eating with Christ in the upper room. It is sometimes called the Breaking of Bread, a name that describes the sacramental action by which Christ is known to disciples. It is sometimes called the Holy Communion, as a reminder of the communion of believers with their Lord and with one another. It is sometimes called the Eucharist or thanksgiving, in which God's people receive with grateful joy the gifts God has prepared for them. In the sacramental action designated by all these names, the Word of God is exhibited and offered to believers.

*Words of Institution*

The Words of Institution set forth the Sacrament as originating in Christ's command, and make plain that those worshiping do so in obedience to God's will. Hereby they participate in the continuing history of the people of God until Christ comes again.

The participation of the entire congregation in the service, as they sing psalms and hymns, offer prayers, and receive the elements, demonstrates that God has redeemed a people and that individuals come to the Table as members of a corporate body.

*The Service of Communion*

The prayers and responses witnessing to the communion of saints testify that the church includes all the faithful everywhere, both in heaven and on earth, and not simply those visibly assembled. The invocation of the Holy Spirit signifies and seeks to ensure that what takes place in the Sacrament is not accomplished by human endeavor, but is done by the grace of God.

**S–3.0500 (New York and Atlanta: Offices of the General Assembly, 1981).

The breaking of the bread and the pouring of the wine show that Christ gave his own body to be broken and his life to be poured out on behalf of humanity, in the offering of himself on the cross. The distribution and partaking of the elements show the reality of believers' union with Christ by faith and their willingness that Christ's presence should abide in them.

The prayers of thanksgiving, the singing of psalms and hymns, and the people's offering of themselves show the response in the praise and self-giving of those who receive the Sacrament.

Let no one presume that words can exhaust the meaning of the Sacrament, but let each one search in the light of the Word of God for further truth God may reveal.

*Time, Place and Frequency*

a. The session shall determine how often the opportunity to partake of the Sacrament may be provided in each church. It is fitting to celebrate the Sacrament as frequently as each Lord's Day, and at least as often as quarterly. Observance should be regular enough that it is seen as a proper part of and not an addition to the worship of God.

*Climax of Public Worship*

Since the Sacrament is an action in which the whole church participates and is a part of the public witness of the church to the power of the Word, it is normally to be celebrated in the regular place of worship as the culmination of the public worship of God. It should not be isolated from the acts of worship which precede and follow it. Thus, it will be preceded properly by the reading and preaching of the Word, during which the people may prepare themselves to receive and appropriate the Word of God offered to them in the Sacrament, that the sacramental Word may be shown forth in full unity with the written and preached Word.

*Special Observances*

b. The session may authorize that the Sacrament be celebrated in connection with the visitation of the sick of that congregation. On such an occasion at least one member of the session, representing the congregation, shall be present in addition to the ministers. A brief exposition of the Word applicable to the circumstances shall be given by the minister so that the Sacrament may be received with understanding.

The session also may authorize the celebration of the Sacrament at other times and places. Such special celebration should be understood to be a part of the public worship of the whole people of God and not a private ceremony. Thus, officers and other members of the congregation should be present along with the minister to demonstrate the communal nature of the Sacrament.

Higher governing bodies of the church also may appoint times for the celebration of the Lord's Supper, either during their sessions or in connection with some gathering of believers which is under their jurisdiction.

*Preparation*

c. Public notice should be given to the congregation at least one week before the celebration of this Sacrament. Either then, or on some other day prior to the administration, the people should be reminded of the nature of the Sacrament and urged to make preparation for it, that all may come in a faithful manner to this Holy Feast.

*Invitation*

d. The minister shall invite to partake of the Sacrament all those who are active church members or communicants in good standing in some Christian church, who trust in the Lord Jesus Christ and repent of their sins, and who covenant anew to live as followers of Christ. The invitation shall include baptized children who are being nurtured and instructed to participate with an understanding of the significance of the invitation to the Lord's Table and of their response in faith.

*Participation*

Participation in the Sacrament is to be understood as a privilege given to the undeserving rather than a right conferred upon the worthy. Yet, those who are unprepared, who are self-sufficient and unrepentant, should be warned not to come to the Holy Table.

*The Elements of the Sacrament*

e. The bread and wine should be made ready well in advance of the celebration. If available, a large piece of bread suitable for breaking and a cup and vessel for pouring the wine should be provided for the minister to use during the Words of Institution. The elements may be placed on the Table and properly covered, or they may be brought forward by members of the church at the appropriate moment during the service.

*Setting Apart*

f. As the Sacrament begins, the minister should set the elements apart by prayer and thanksgiving, which shall include remembrance of the death and resurrection of Christ, and shall ask that the Holy Spirit sanctify the Sacrament to the people's benefit.

*Administration of the Sacrament*

g. When the time for the administration of the Sacrament has come the minister shall show:

1. By reading the Words of Institution, either from the Gospels or from First Corinthians, that our Lord Jesus has commanded this Sacrament to be observed in the church; thereby showing the Lord's death till he comes;

2. That it is for the perpetual remembrance of the sacrifice of Jesus Christ, for the sealing of all the benefits of Christ's death and resurrection to all true believers, for their spiritual nourishment and growth and for their further dedication to the loving service which they owe to God;

3. That it is a bond and pledge of their communion with Christ and with each other, as members of Christ's body.

The minister shall take bread and break it in the view of the people, saying:

> Our Lord Jesus Christ, on the same night in which he was betrayed, having taken bread, and blessed and broken it, gave it to his disciples; as I, ministering in his name, give this bread to you; saying, "Take, eat; this is my body, which is broken for you; this do in remembrance of me." (Here the bread is to be distributed.)

Following the giving of the bread, the minister shall take the cup, pour wine into it, and say:

> After the same manner our Savior also took the cup, and having given thanks, as has been done in his name, he gave it to the disciples, saying, "This cup is the New Testament in my blood, which is shed for many, for the remission of sins: all of you drink of it." (Here the wine is to be distributed.)

*Distribution*

h. If the people do not gather at the Table, the elements are to be taken to them in their pews by elders. Inactive elders may be invited to serve, and when there is an insufficient number of elders available, deacons or other church members may be invited by the minister and session to serve in distributing the elements.

*Personal Communion*

Since believers are to act personally in their commitment to the Lord, it is proper that a part of the time occupied in the distribution of the elements should be spent by all in communion with God, confession, thanksgiving, intercession, and in renewing the believer's personal covenant with the Lord.

*Conclusion of the Sacrament*

i. After the distribution and partaking of the elements, the service may continue with prayers which include thanks to God for the great gifts received in the Sacrament, and prayers for the church and for communion with the saints, that all who truly are Christ's may one day join together in giving Christ all praise and honor. The congregation should sing a psalm or hymn, and be dismissed with a benediction.

*Offering*

j. It is appropriate, in connection with the celebration of the Lord's Supper, to receive an offering designated for some special purpose. These offerings shall be received at such times as ordered by the session.

APPENDIX 6

# OFFICE AND ORDINATION IN THE REFORMED TRADITION

Paul R. Fries

## INTRODUCTION

The task of this paper is to provide an account of office and ordination which will help Lutherans understand the theology and practice of ministry in churches of the Reformed tradition. Neither a historical investigation nor a theological analysis will be attempted. The following will be primarily reportorial in character.

The method employed will be to examine the liturgies and books of church order used by several denominations holding presbyterial forms of government and from this to develop a composite sketch of office and ordination. Even so uncomplicated a method, however, raises several points requiring comment at the outset.

The first pertains to the scope of this investigation. The inquiry which follows is restricted to office and ordination in churches using the presbyterial system of government. The term Reformed, of course, is properly more inclusive than this. The Reformed pedigree of the congregational tradition, for example, is not being challenged here; the polity of congregational churches represents a sub-tradition, however, which could be adequately treated only in a much longer study. Similarly, the order of the United Church of Christ has not been examined in this paper, not because it lacks features that would qualify it as Reformed, but because it represents a special development in church history and would therefore require a separate treatment.

The second point is more substantive. When examining formulations concerning the office of minister of the word found in the liturgies and books of church order currently used by churches of the Reformed tradition, it becomes clear that these documents sound a somewhat different tone concerning the pastoral office from that of earlier explications. The classical Reformed understanding of the minister of the word centers in the relation of this office to the means of grace by which salvation is mediated to the people of God, i.e., the word and sacraments. When "The Order for the Ordination and Installation of a Minister or a Missionary" in the *Liturgy and Psalms* of the Reformed

Church in America (RCA), after citing Matt. 16:19 (power of the keys), states that "The office of the Christian Ministry is both glorious and necessary, and the Lord will have such an office always to remain . . . ," the point of such high sounding language is not to elevate the minister or even the office. It is rather to underscore that the pastoral office is an instrument freely chosen by God and empowered through the Holy Spirit to serve the gospel of Jesus Christ.

This "soteric-instrumental" understanding of the pastoral office, as it will be called in this paper, has been overlaid in current Reformed order by another concept of ministry. Today the formulations used by most Presbyterian and Reformed congregations in the United States present a view of ministry that begins with the call to service of the entire people of God and develops an understanding of the pastoral office on the basis of this broader call to ministry. The pastor is presented in this view as one who equips and enables the people of God for its ministry. The function is distinct, but the ministry is shared. This understanding of ministry will be referred to as "missional-functional."

The "missional-functional" view is deeply rooted in the Reformed tradition, even though it has been developed and more fully introduced into the life of the church in our century. The foundation for the "missional-functional" understanding is found in the dual Reformation doctrines of the priesthood of all believers and Christian vocation (see the Joint Statement on Ministry in this report). These doctrines have combined with the twentieth-century rediscovery of the ministry of the laity and the identification of the church as existing for mission in the world to produce the articulation of the pastoral office described here. To speak then, of a "missional-functional" overlay on the older "soteric-instrumental" view of the pastoral office is not to suggest that a novel understanding of ministry has developed, but rather that new emphases have emerged without negating previous ones.

To identify shifting emphases in the understanding and practice of ministry calls to mind a foundational principle of the Reformed tradition, namely, that no human interpretation or practice is immutable; every aspect of the life and teaching of the church is subject to continuing reformation according to the word of God. New light from Scripture may well demand changes in the theology and practice of the church. In regard to the matter of office and ordination, however, the issue of change and development goes even beyond this principle of continuing reformation. From the time of Calvin, Reformed theologians have acknowledged that more than one understanding of form and function may be consistent with scriptural teaching concerning the *ministerium*. The notion of the continuing reformation of the teaching and practices of the church combines with the acknowledgement that Scripture does not speak a definitive word on the matter of order to produce a large measure of flexibility in Reformed discussions of office and ordination.

This does not mean that Reformed commentators have viewed ministerial order and function as merely a pragmatic issue, nor that Scripture has nothing relevant to say about it. Scripture speaks clearly enough about the necessity of the proclamation of the word and the administration of the sacraments. There is no ambiguity in its message calling for the nurturing, guiding, encouraging, admonishing, instructing, and training of the people of God. The biblical word concerning the spiritual, emotional, and physical care of those who belong to the household of faith is plainly spoken. And although we have been slow to hear it, the scriptural call that the entire people of God be equipped to engage its ministry in the world is sounded clearly by Scripture. Office and ordination are issues which Reformed Christians find enormously important. But they believe that the *ministerium* must be subservient to the purposes of God for the church and to its mission in the world. Form, content, and function must follow divine purpose and mission—and not the reverse.

The key word, then, when seeking to understand office and ordination in the Reformed tradition is freedom. God freely chooses to employ human agents in the ministry of reconciliation. We are free from the tyranny of an absolute order to shape, under the guidance of the word, government and office in such a way that in each generation God's purpose and mission will be well-served. In such freedom is located the hope of both the church and the world it serves.

## 1. THE NATURE, POWER, AND AUTHORITY OF OFFICE IN REFORMED PRACTICE

Current Reformed faith and practice concerning ordination is anchored in a theological understanding of the church and its ministry admirably summarized in the "Report of the Joint Taskforce on the Nature and Practice of Ministry" (UPCUSA and PCUS before reunion): ". . . there is one call of God to the whole church and to every member to the ministry of Jesus Christ in the world, with office in the church being calling to certain functions in the church."*

The movement is thus not from God in Christ to ordained ministers to the people, but from God in Christ to the whole baptized people, and then to the ordained ministry. "There is one call of God . . . to the mission and ministry of God's word and work in Jesus Christ. Those who hear and respond to this call through baptism and commissioning share in God's mission . . ." (UPCUSA *BO* 36.01). But "while the ministry is one, specific forms of ministry may emphasize special tasks and skills . . ." (PC[U.S.A.] *BO* G–6.0104). The traditional three offices of the Reformed tradition (minister of the word, ruling elder, deacon) are in this missional-functional view interpreted in terms of the specialized service offered through them. They are not to be regarded as a priori to the ministry of the whole people of God; the reverse is true, that ministry being seen as the a priori of ordained ministry.

As is true of the call to ministry, the authority of office derives from Jesus Christ. The *BO* of the PC(U.S.A.) states: "His ministry is the basis of all ministries . . ." (G–6.0101). The *BCO* of the RCA speaks of this authority as being of three kinds: ministerial (the right to act for Christ), declarative (the right to speak in his name), and spiritual (the right to govern the affairs of the church) (*BCO*, p. 9).

In a section dating back to 1788, the *BO* of the PC(U.S.A.) speaks of ministerial and declarative power, insisting that "Holy Scriptures are the only rule of faith and manners" (G–1.0307). Here we see the classic Reformed understanding of power and authority in the church: Jesus Christ, head of the church, delegates power to the offices, but only insofar as the office holders are faithful servants of the word.

The line of progression in these sections seems to move from Christ to the word, from the word to the ordained servants of the word, and finally to the people of God, and they thus give expression to the earlier soteric-instrumental concept of ordained ministry. The *BCO* of the RCA tries to blend this older notion of office with the missional-functional one it came to express after 1968 by distinguishing power from authority. It argues that while the Holy Spirit gives to the entire people of God the power Christ bestows, the church cannot properly serve

*The material in this section is drawn, except where otherwise indicated, from the *Worshipbook* used by the Cumberland Presbyterian Church and the PC(U.S.A.), the PC(U.S.A.) *BO*, the *Liturgy and Psalms* of the RCA, the RCA *BCO*. Because not all of the official documents of the recently formed PC(U.S.A.) (representing the reunion of the United Presbyterian Church in the U.S.A. and the Presbyterian Church in the United States) are now easily available, the *BO* of the UPCUSA is also used.

him without order, organization, and government; and consequently it is necessary that some be given authority over others (p. 8). Note that the ground of the authority of the office is Christ's pneumatological presence with the entire people, thus establishing a functional, but not essential, interpretation of authority. The offices represent Christ through the people before they represent Christ to the people.

The implication of this is that in current presbyterial order there is a relative parity among the offices. The word "relative" is used because the documents under consideration continue, it seems, to give a certain priority to the minister of the word and elder over that of the deacon. (See the PC[U.S.A.] *BO* G–6.0407 for the provision whereby a congregation may choose not to employ the office of deacon.) Yet the intention is to place the offices of the church on the same plane, the one exercising authority over the other only on the basis of function. (See, for example, the ordination service in the *Worshipbook* where no distinction except in task is made.) The notion of the parity of offices, while present in classical Reformed theology, has been given significant expansion by the functional-missional polity of the modern church.

The relative parity of the ordained ministries is closely related to a venerable doctrine of Reformed ecclesiology, namely, the complementarity of the offices. While the term itself is obviously a modern one, the concept of the three offices participating in the soteric economy goes back to Bucer and Calvin. The theological ground for this derives from the understanding that ordained ministers have no original power or authority but only channel what is given by Christ, the Lord of the church. "The principle of equality of the ministry, conceived now in its broadest sense as including the functions of the elder and the deacon, is based upon the fact that the entire ministerial or pastoral office is summed up in Jesus Christ himself. . . . Every ministerial function is found preeminently in him. By his Holy Spirit he distributes those functions among those who he calls to serve in his name" (RCA *BCO*, Preamble, p. 9). In regard to the order of the church, the ministry of Christ is not continued in one office but three.

## 2. THE TASKS OF THE ORDAINED OFFICES

What is the unique contribution of each office to that ministry? The office of deacon "is one of sympathy, witness, and service, after the example of Jesus Christ" (PC[U.S.A.] *BO* G–6.0401). Deacons are "ministers of God's love and mercy . . ." (RCA, *Liturgy and Psalms*, p.

110); they are called to lead the congregation to help the friendless and needy and show the love and justice of Christ in their ministry (*Worshipbook,* Cumberland and PC[U.S.A.]). In the ordination service of the RCA the deacon is charged with the financial administration of the church, the care of the sick, visitation of the distressed, and the disposition of benevolent concerns in general. The deacon is also to give aid to the congregation during services of worship. Although it is not specified in the *Liturgy* or *BCO* of the RCA, deacons usually assume responsibility for the physical resources of the church. This was explicit in the *BO* of the UPCUSA, which charged deacons not only to devise "effective methods of collecting the gifts of the people," but also to take responsibility for the finances and properties of the church and for "its evangelistic, missionary, and educational programs" as well if these duties were delegated to them by the session (40.05). These tasks are not mentioned in the *BO* of the PC(U.S.A.), but neither are they precluded (G–6.0402). In both the RCA and the PC(U.S.A.) deacons may form their own board. Deacons are part of the consistory of the RCA, but not of the session of the PC(U.S.A.); in neither denomination do they serve on the higher judicatories. They are ordained in the local congregation through the laying on of hands by the minister of the church in the RCA and the session in the PC(U.S.A.).

The office of the ruling elder has been described as the glory of the Reformed tradition. Together with the minister of the word, elders supervise the congregations of which they are part. In the Presbyterian churches elders join ministers to form the session which governs the congregation (in the RCA deacons are included, and the governing body is known as the consistory). Pastoral concerns are shared by the elder. "They have charge of all matters relating to the welfare and good order of the church. They have oversight over the conduct of the members of the congregation and seek to bring that conduct into conformity with the Word of God" (RCA *BCO,* Chap. 1, Part I, Article 1, Sec. 7). The following quotation from the *BO* of the UPCUSA eloquently states the elder's call to pastoral responsibility:

> Ruling elders should also visit the people in their homes, especially the sick; they should instruct the ignorant, comfort the mourner, nourish and guard the children of the church; and all those duties which private Christians are bound to discharge by the law of love are especially incumbent upon them by divine vocation, and are to be discharged as official duties; they should pray with and for the people; they should be careful and diligent in seeking the fruit of the preached Word among the flock; and should inform the pastor in cases of sickness, affliction, and awakening,

and of all others which may need special attention from the pastor. They should, moreover, cultivate zealously their aptness to teach the Bible and should improve every opportunity of doing so, to the end that destitute places, mission points, and churches without pastors may be supplied with religious services (39.04). (See also PC(U.S.A.) *BO* G–6.0304, G–10.0101–2.)

While in both churches the elders are given the responsibility of assuring that services of worship are regularly conducted and the word of God is preached and taught, the delineation of the duties of the elder in the order of the RCA includes certain elements not clearly stated in that of the PC(U.S.A.) In both elders are charged with the spiritual oversight of the congregation, but in the RCA also with the supervision of the preaching and teaching of the minister of the word. "The elders are particularly enjoined to have regard to the teaching . . . of the minister of the Word, to the end that all things be directed to the upbuilding of the church, and that no strange doctrine be taught" (*Liturgy and Psalms*, p. 108). This responsibility was at one time undertaken with great seriousness in the churches of the Dutch Reformation as is illustrated by the practice which has disappeared in the RCA in this country. The service began when the board of elders filed into the nave, followed by the minister, to take its place in a special bank of pews while the minister ascended to the pulpit. After the pronouncement of the benediction, the minister descended from the pulpit as the senior elder rose to meet him. An extended hand told the minister and congregation that the sermon was regarded as doctrinally sound; a withheld handshake represented the refusal of the senior elder's imprimatur. The practice has disappeared, but the responsibility of the elder for sound teaching yet remains. The minister alone is not responsible for the purity of the preached word. While the *BO* of the PC(U.S.A.) does not specify that the elder monitor the preaching and teaching of the minister, the session's responsibility for sound preaching and teaching is emphatically asserted (G–10.0102, c).

The elder in the Reformed tradition has historically stood as guardian not only of the preached and taught word but of the sacraments as well. The liturgy of the RCA instructs elders "to prevent as much as possible the sacraments from being profaned." Note that the authority of the elder is thus established vis à vis the congregation (in contrast to the guardianship of the word which is directed primarily toward the minister). At issue here is the exercise of discipline within the congregation; the source of the profanation of the sacraments is located in the faithlessness and sinful behavior of the congregants rather than in the manner in which the sacraments are administered. Thus the elder is charged not only with determining who is to be numbered in the community formed around word and sacrament but also with responsibility for reformation of the behavior of the congregation. Elders are as important in their own way as the minister of the word for the proper celebration of the Lord's Supper. And since the gospel calls the believer to faithfulness and obedience in all of life, the secular as well as the sacred, the office of elder has historically played an important role in what today would be called the mission of the church in the world. The elder is ordained by the session in the PC(U.S.A.) and by the minister of the congregation in the RCA. In both Reformed and Presbyterian churches elders must be equally represented with ministers on the higher judicatories and are eligible to be elected to the offices of these judicatories.

The third office recognized in the Reformed tradition is that of the minister of the word. The minister of the word has been called a teaching elder, such a designation underscoring the unity of this office with that of the ruling elder. "The Reformed churches consider the minister of the Word to be an elder of a special kind, called in some churches of the Reformed order the 'teaching elder.' Ministers and elders, therefore, govern the church together" (RCA *BCO*, p. 9). The function of this office, however, is larger than suggested by such a designation. Again the *BO* of the former UPCUSA speaks eloquently (cf. PC[U.S.A.] *BO* G–6.0202):

> The person who fulfills this responsibility has, in Scripture, obtained different names expressive of his or her various duties. As he or she has the oversight of the flock of Christ he or she is termed bishop. As he or she feeds them with spiritual food he or she is termed pastor. As a servant of Christ in the Church the term minister is given. As it is his or her duty to be grave and prudent, and an example to the flock, and to govern well in the house and Kingdom of Christ, he or she is termed presbyter or elder. As he or she is sent to declare the will of God to sinners, and to beseech them to be reconciled to God, through Christ, he or she is termed ambassador. And as he or she dispenses the manifold grace of God and the ordinances instituted by Christ, he or she is termed steward of the mysteries of God. (38.02)

The responsibilities of the minister of the word are threefold according to the liturgy of the RCA: to proclaim the gospel and teach the Scripture; to administer the sacraments; and to govern the church through Christian discipline (the so-called power of the keys, Matt. 16:19). While the liturgy of the PC(U.S.A.) reflects these three areas in its interrogation of the candidate for ordination (without referring to discipline as the power of the keys, however), it also requires that the ministers show the "love and justice of Jesus Christ." In the missional-functional perspective, emphasis is laid on the responsibility of the minister to enable and equip the people of God for its mission in the world. The minister as an instrument in the pneumatological mediation of grace through word and sacrament may be underplayed in contemporary Reformed order. But that is a matter which cannot be addressed here. The minister presides over the session or consistory and is a member of a presbytery or classis (regional units governing a number of churches). He or she is also eligible to serve as a delegate to and hold office in the higher judicatories. The church at every level is governed by ministers and elders. The minister of the word is ordained by the classis or presbytery; in the case of the RCA ministers of the ordaining classis alone lay hands on the ordained; in the PC(U.S.A.) both the elders and ministers of the presbytery participate.

## 3. THE CANDIDATE FOR OFFICE

Let us now turn from the matter of the concept and purpose of office and address another concern of Reformed order: the person to be ordained to office. The qualifications for ordination may be described under three headings: the candidate must be called, gifted, and when necessary trained.

The discussion may be brief here. The call of God is spoken in two ways according to the liturgy of the RCA. Elders and deacons are asked during the service of ordination if they ". . . feel in (their) hearts that (they) are lawfully called of God's Church, and therefore of God himself, to (their) respected offices?" The *Worshipbook* of the PC(U.S.A.) does not speak of the inner call, but only of God's call "by the voice of the church." In both churches gifts for a particular ministry are seen as a presupposition of the call to ministry and eventual ordination. Finally, the educational requirements for ministers of the word are meticulously attended to in the PC(U.S.A.) and RCA. Although the nature of the training of elders and deacons is not prescribed, the offering of some sort of training program is common in congregations of the Reformed family of churches. The PC(U.S.A.) calls for elders to study and be examined by the session concerning "their personal faith; knowledge of the doctrine, government, and discipline contained in the Constitution of the church; and the duties of the office" (PC[U.S.A.] *BO* G–14.0205).

## 4. ORDINATION

To this point the approach to the question of ordination in the Reformed tradition has been to explicate the doctrine of office presented in those primary documents which determine order in the RCA and PC(U.S.A.). The discussion has examined the concept of office, the function of the offices, and the qualification of the candidates for office. It may have been noted that while the question of ordination per se has never been far from this discussion, neither has it been addressed directly. This procedure has been followed for the simple reason that this is precisely the manner in which the documents under consideration present ordination, that is, by discussing office and the office holder rather than the meaning of the act itself.

The *BO* of the PC(U.S.A.) did in fact include a chapter on the doctrine of ordination (16). It is a short chapter of only three paragraphs. It can easily be quoted in its entirety:

1. Those who have been called to the office of minister, ruling elder or deacon in the Church are to be inducted by ordination.
2. Ordination is the authoritative admission of those duly called to these offices in the Church of God, accompanied with prayer and the laying on of hands, to which it is proper to add the giving of the right hand of fellowship.
3. Each of these offices is, according to the Scriptures, a special charge, and no person shall be ordained unless it be to the performance of a definite work.

The *BCO* of the RCA falls short of even this abbreviated treatment. Speaking of the ordination of a minister of the word, it provides only practical instruction: "That service shall be conducted by the classis in regular or special session with proper solemnity. A sermon suitable to the occasion shall be preached, and the promises, directions, explanations of duty, and the laying on of hands shall be according to . . . the church's *Liturgy*" (Chap. 1, Part II, Article 10, Sec. 5). In the ordination service of the RCA as well as that of PC(U.S.A.), little which might deepen our understanding of the meaning of this ritual act is added. The enlightenment and strengthening of the ordained by the Holy Spirit is prayed for, a declaration is made, the support of the congregation and classis is pledged.

The Reformed tradition, while clearly wishing to continue the ancient practice of ordination with the laying on of hands, has not invested this act with the richness of theological meaning that has developed around the doctrine of office.

In conclusion, it seems safe to say that the understanding of the *ministerium* with a threefold office which has characterized Reformed policy will probably be continued for the forseeable future in most churches. This polity has proved faithful and holds promise for the future. At the same time it cannot be said that the definitive Reformed order has been achieved. Such an order cannot exist. To the degree that it is faithful to the Lord it serves, order too will be in a constant process of change and renewal. That is, or at least should be, the first and last word concerning office and ordination in the Reformed tradition.

## APPENDIX 7

# CHURCH AND MINISTRY*

WARREN A. QUANBECK

## 1. THE MINISTRY OF THE ENTIRE PEOPLE OF GOD

Discussion of the Christian ministry in our day is determined by two important factors: historical studies in the Scriptures and in the development of theology, and the development in doctrinal discussion and common study of the Scriptures in the ecumenical movement. The impact of these two factors is great, bringing about important changes in the way the Christian ministry is viewed and evaluated.

The impact of historical studies is to make clear that there is no one form of structuring the ministry of the church which has clear divine sanction. The church has at various times in its history adapted different structures to the service of the gospel, frequently using the structures available in the culture to which it was ministering. In the course of its history the church has used congregational, presbyterial, and episcopal polities, with numerous variations and combinations of them.

The most significant impact of the ecumenical discussion of the ministry is the insistence that the ministry of the church properly refers to the ministry of all Christians in the world and not merely to the service of a special group of people set aside by ordination. The entire people of God have a mission in and for the world, a mission which is a continuation or projection of the mission of Jesus Christ. Its dimensions correspond to his mission also, proclaiming the good news of God's kingly rule, embodying God's love in the service of his creatures, offering up in union with Jesus Christ the true worship of God, offering forgiveness to sinners, reconciliation to the alienated, redemption to captives, and cleansing, healing, and restoration to those maimed, crippled, or ravaged by disease.

The entire people of God is called to this ministry. Baptism is the ordination or consecration of the Christian to this calling. In baptism the believer is united with Christ in his self-giving for humankind and participates in his death and resurrection. The believer's entire life as a Christian is the living out of this relationship. Life in the people of God is both equipment for and exercise of this mission, which can take a

*A study prepared for a consultation held 20–21 September 1971, in Chicago by the Division of Theological Studies of the Lutheran Council in the U.S.A.

variety of forms and functions depending upon the kind of gifts entrusted to a person by God and upon that person's role in the family and society.

The people of God, moreover, is called to this ministry not only as a group of individuals but as a community. The congregation is not only motivator of the individual's service in the world but makes its own distinctive contribution as the worshipping, witnessing, and serving community. It proclaims the message of reconciliation and also exemplifies its message in reconciling human beings to God and to each other. It makes the love of God believable by deeds of love. Through prophetic interpretation of the word of God it helps the world to comprehend the purpose of God as well as the true meaning of human life. Through its worship it witnesses to the theological dimension of the world and of human life. Through opposition to evil, oppression, and injustice it authenticates the good news to the poor and disinherited.

This mission of the people of God has several aspects: worship, witness, service, and often suffering.

In its worship God's people exercise in union with Jesus Christ the praise of and obedience to God which Christ offered in his mission to humankind. The Christian community remembers the redeeming acts through which God offers life to the world and whose recollection by the church is the continuing source of its self-awareness and renewal. It hears the word of God which judges the human striving for autonomy but which also announces God's redemption of humankind in the cross and resurrection of Christ. It discovers anew the meaning of reconciliation with God and with each other and the Christian calling to be agents of reconciliation to humankind. It experiences the community which overcomes loneliness and alienation and is sensitized to the needs of human beings and society. The maintenance of a regular schedule of services of worship reminds Christians and all humankind that no human is self-sufficient but each needs the theological dimension of a relationship with God. In its worship and proclamation the community seeks to interpret the will of God in Christ for the life situation in which it lives.

As Jesus Christ is the "faithful witness," so his people bear witness to the reality of God, his sovereignty as creator, his providential care for and constant renewal of his creation, his redemptive love in Christ, his power as Holy Spirit, and his unrelenting pursuit of his purpose for fellowship with his creatures. The church bears witness by its proclamation of the gospel, by its interpretation of the will of God to the situations and issues of its day, and by its existence in the world as a worshipping and serving community. As custodian of the Scriptures and heir of rich traditions of creed, liturgy, devotion, and discipline, the church has the constant task of renewing and deepening its understanding of the gospel and its self-awareness as a community of witness in the world.

The people of God are in the world as Jesus Christ was, not to be served but to serve and to offer up its life for the sake of the world. The church is not in the world merely as ark of salvation or as most privileged people, but as instrument of God's redemptive purpose for his creation. Through Christ and his body the church, God is not merely conducting a rescue operation but asserting his sovereign lordship and beginning even now his loving conquest of humankind and his victory through obedience and suffering over the forces of evil. The worship and witness of God's people is a part of this service and so is its attention to the needs of human beings and society, its work of reconciliation, its service to the hungry, the poor, the sick, and the disinherited. At times the service of the church to the world involves suffering, whether through persecution or because of loyalty to Christ through identification with underprivileged or despised people. In some situations the people of God may be so restricted in their expression of their faith that patient acceptance of oppression and suffering becomes their most potent witness and service. Christians who can accept such situations without bitterness or self-pity make a gracious contribution to the fellowship of God's people all over the world.

By its service to the world the Christian community testifies to God's concern for the world and to its dignity and worth as God's creation. It insists that God's judgment upon sin and evil does not mean rejection of the world but rather his will for its renewal. The cross and resurrection of Christ are not only good news for individuals but a declaration that God is reclaiming the environment for his purpose of community in love. The people of God are not refugees from some cosmic disaster but a task force for the rehabilitation of the creation. Christians make a realistic appraisal of the depth and extent of evil in the world but nevertheless make an optimistic prognosis for the creation. They speak not of an escape of Christians into immortality while the world sinks into ruin, but hold out the hope of a new heaven and a new earth. They serve the world with joy and confidence, knowing that it is a world over which Christ reigns as Savior and Lord.

The mission of the people of God corresponds to the mission of Christ also in its glad acceptance of the servant form. Christians must acknowledge with pain and sorrow the triumphalism and ecclesiastical imperialism which have darkened the pages of the church's history. They must also acknowledge the way in which Christians have patronized and at times even bullied their fellow human beings. The alliance between the church and the imperial authorities over more than a millennium has obscured the gospel of God's love and falsified the role of the church in the world. The recognition that God's kingly rule is revealed to us in Christ the servant of humankind reminds us that we too are called to a ministry of service. We must respect the dignity and freedom of all human beings and acknowledge the validity of all cultures as media for the gospel and for structures of Christian service. We must acknowledge that we are all called to service and that our true dignity is to be found not in the titles or ranks that impress popular opinion but in correspondence to him who emptied himself, took the form of a servant, and who will one day be acknowledged by all as King of kings and Lord of lords.

The Lutheran church has spoken of the church as the community of the word of God. It has understood this to mean that the church is the result of God's revelatory initiative in Israel and in Christ, that it lives by the proclamation of the word concerning Jesus Christ, and that it lives for the communication of the word of God to the world. The climactic manifestation of the word of God is the ministry of Jesus Christ, whose mission provides the fullest exemplification of the Old Testament prophets' conviction that the word of God is also the deed of God. The manifestation of the word of God in the Christian community is another manifestation of this. The church is the body of Christ, the visible manifestation of Christ in the world. Its very existence is for the sake of revealing Christ as God's deed for the world. Its proclamation is a communication of Christ the word of God; its sacraments are dramatic liturgical presentations of Christ the living Word; its worship, witness, and service seek to present, render credible, and authenticate God's presence in Christ for the reconciliation of humankind.

## 2. SPECIAL MINISTRY

In order that the people of God may carry out their mission in and for the world God has given them gifts of ministry, whose task it is to equip and motivate for mission. Thus within the mission or ministry of the entire people of God there is a special ministry which serves the people of God in its mission. In one sense this ordained ministry is a part of the people of God, united with them in the task of mission, and standing with them beneath the judgment and grace of God. In another sense the ordained ministry stands on behalf of Christ over against the people of God, entrusted with the exposition of the word of God, and presiding over the sacraments as representatives of Christ whose action the sacraments are, equipping and exhorting the people of God to be what they are in Jesus Christ for their mission. The function of leadership and encouragement should not be understood on the analogy of leadership in the civil community but on the analogy of Christ's servanthood. The history of the church abounds in painful examples of failure to make this elementary observation, where church leadership has been domineering, proud, unscrupulous, and patronizing. Movements of renewal in all church groups urge us to conform to the servant image more consistently in order that the ordained ministry in the church may indeed represent Jesus Christ in the equipment of the saints for ministry.

The gifts of the Spirit to the people of God are of different kinds for different needs of the community. The apostles of Jesus Christ are witnesses of the resurrection and founders of the Christian community. Prophets have the task of interpreting the word of God out of its matrix in past revelatory events to the new situations confronting the apostolic community. The pastor tends the flock of God, nourishing them with their proper food and protecting them against their enemies. The other gifts—teacher, healer, administrator, speaker in tongues, interpreter of tongues—all have their appropriate roles in the healthy functioning of the body. The fact that the gifts are not the same in the various lists in the New Testament may be an indication of incompleteness of enumeration or may indicate that different situations call for different gifts and perhaps also different structures of community. The fact that the church has both in the New Testament and in subsequent history utilized various structures to serve its needs at different times suggests that the people of God has responsible freedom to develop the functions and structures it needs for effective work in its mission.

By contrast to the diverse ministries of the early church the ministry of word and sacrament of the Lutheran church in history seems monolithic and narrow. The long shadow of the medieval concept of priesthood has in fact made Lutheran practice with respect to the ordained ministry less flexible and adaptable than it could have been. But if we understand the ministry of word and sacrament in terms of the New Testament understanding of revelation or of Luther's understanding of the way God works in coming to his people, a great deal of flexibility becomes apparent. The ordained minister then appears as one who serves the media which God has chosen to effect his gracious presence among humankind, and whatever serves the grace of God in this way is a legitimate, ordained ministry. The most common form of ordained ministry will no doubt continue to be that of servant of the word and sacraments in a local congregation, but any ministry which the church needs in its situation to effect God's gracious presence is possible: missionaries, chaplaincies, counselors, teachers, administrators, and so on.

The function of this ordained ministry is thus to assist the Christian community to effect its mission in Christ on his behalf. It is a special ministry of leadership in the model of Christ's servanthood, of motivation, inspiration, guidance, and care. In different social and cultural situations different aspects of this special ministry may be more important than others: in the early church's struggle with misunderstanding of the gospel and heresy, theological leadership was a chief desideratum; in time of persecution, courage, patience, and readiness to suffer on behalf of Christ were required of leadership. In our day the different cultural situations of the Christian community make different demands upon this ordained ministry. In countries where the church is restricted or persecuted, the demand is for a wise and courageous witness. In countries where the indigenous church is just emerging, the need is for encouragement and sustaining new leadership and for gracious stepping aside. In the West one of the great needs seems to be that of helping congregations and synods to adjust to rapid social changes so as not to seem merely custodians of the past or opponents of anything new or different.

## 3. THE RECOGNITION OF THE ORDAINED MINISTRY

From earliest times the Christian community has recognized the working of the ministerial gifts of the Spirit in its midst by a ritual act involving the imposition of hands and prayer for the guidance and power of the Spirit upon the person so set aside. The imposition of hands has been understood as a sign of recognition that the person is indeed called by the Spirit to a distinctive service in the Christian community and as a sign that the congregation is praying that the Spirit may grant wisdom and power in carrying out the ministry. This rite has been traditionally designated ordination, and in most Christian traditions is the accepted form by which persons are received and set apart for this ministry in the church. The theological interpretation of the rite has differed: in the Orthodox and Catholic traditions and by some Anglicans it is regarded as a sacrament bestowing a special gift of grace; Lutherans have been reluctant to designate it as a sacrament, although their confessional books do so in one place.

Ordination in the Lutheran tradition has been seen as the act by which a person is set apart for the ministry of word and sacrament in the Christian community. The rite does not bestow a higher status upon the person ordained. That person remains a servant of the gospel and a member of the ministering community. Nor does ordination effect any ontological change in the ordained, who remains a redeemed sinner but with special responsibility for the service of God among God's people.

What ordination does accomplish is the recognition of a person having a special task within the mission of the entire community, a task that provides leadership, motivation, or encouragement for the community in its Christian responsibility. It recognizes the specific character of the task within the community and the relationship of that task to God's self-giving to his people in word and sacrament. The ordained are not professional in the sense that they alone know the secrets of the Christian mission nor, hopefully, in the sense that they are mere functionaries who keep the prayer-wheel turning. But they should be professional in the sense that they have competence for assigned functions, that they know how to relate to human needs, understand the bearing of the love of God upon specific situations, and have been educated to openness to persons and to the needs to society.

Ordination is therefore an appropriate recognition by the church for a position which serves the self-giving of God to his people in word and sacrament and which provides leadership and assistance to the Christian community in its mission in and for the world.

For centuries the church has spoken both of sending and calling with reference to ordained ministry. "Sending" is the language of the missionary community and expresses the conviction that if a certain work needs to be done, the church has the right and indeed the obligation to send someone to do it. "Calling" is the language of the established congregation which reaches outside its own membership for someone to do a specific task. In modern times churches have been able to use both vocabularies in speaking of the ordained ministry. We send missionaries, teachers, and chaplains, and we ordain them for these tasks. We do so readily and without question if the work is done with a clear relationship to the word of God and the sacraments. We are reluctant to do so if this relationship is not apparent or if the work does not have some direct bearing upon the church's task of carrying out its mission in the world.

# A STATEMENT OF LUTHERANS TO LUTHERANS REFLECTING ON THIS DIALOGUE

We encourage a careful reading of both the text of the report of this Lutheran-Reformed dialogue and of the generous notes that have been provided for those who wish to explore more thoroughly the issues that we have discussed with our Reformed brothers and sisters. This is especially important because of the long time that has elapsed since Lutherans and Reformed began official theological conversation in North America almost twenty years ago and because of the lack of broad study by or response from our churches to the official reports and recommendations from the two dialogues.[1]

Since that first dialogue, which was published in 1966 under the title *Marburg Revisited*, Lutherans in North America have been in dialogue with Methodists, Conservative Evangelicals, Baptists, Orthodox, Roman Catholics, and Episcopalians. These last two dialogues have asked the sponsoring churches for action. Lutheran-Episcopal Dialogue II resulted in the mutual declaration that both Lutheran and Episcopal churches are "churches in which the Gospel is preached and taught," and in formal "encouragement of development of common Christian life throughout the respective churches."[2]

These are exciting times of opening windows and doors to other Christian communities. Common ground and experience in the faith is being identified. Common issues of ministry and mission are being identified in our setting in North America. We are learning to know and appreciate the richness and uniqueness of other traditions, and we have been given the opportunity to share the richness and uniqueness of our Lutheran tradition.

The goal of all of our dialogue efforts is to manifest the unity of the church of Jesus Christ. Each dialogue, depending on the degree of convergence or consensus reached and depending on reception by the churches, becomes a move toward a realization of that unity to which we are all called.

We discriminate carefully between "unity" and "organic union" (which might be achieved by merger). We do not believe it to be possible or desirable that all Christian communions should become identical. While we recognize that unity does indeed have implications for organic union, it is not the latter that this report is proposing.

But we do testify to our conviction that, when Lutheran criteria for unity are recognized in the Confessions and the life of another church, ecclesiastical integrity compels us to make public affirmation of this, to eat the Lord's Supper together, and to welcome common efforts in ministry and mission.

Each theological dialogue in which Lutherans have participated has given to the participants and the churches opportunity to understand and appreciate the heritage and the present living witness of other Christian communions. Stereotypes are identified and often dissipated. Common grounds in the faith are celebrated. Our unfamiliarity with the actual traditions and present practice of others is often embarrassing. We all have much to learn as we grow together toward the unity that Christ gives us, a unity which is of the very nature of the church.

Others have engaged in this task before us.

We therefore committed two full days of this dialogue series to a detailed review of the summary statements and the conclusion of *Marburg Revisited.* We had opportunity to study the Reformed Confessions and to reexamine our own. We were able to take no exception to the summary statements and the conclusion, though we recognize that, almost two decades later, we have become accustomed to a new ecumenical vocabulary which provides substantial assistance in transcending some of the historic polarizing slogans.

It is important that Lutherans hear, almost twenty years later, the conclusion of that first Lutheran-Reformed dialogue:

> A number of differing views and emphases remain to be resolved, but we are encouraged to believe that further contacts will lead to further agreement between the churches here represented. *We regard none of these remaining differences to be of sufficient consequence to prevent fellowship. We have recognized in each other's teachings a common understanding of the Gospel and have concluded that the issues which divide the two major branches of the Reformation can no longer be regarded as constituting obstacles to mutual understanding and fellowship.*[3]

We are delighted to repeat and reaffirm this statement which was endorsed by the Lutheran participants, including Conrad Bergendoff, Herbert J. A. Bouman, George W. Forell, Martin H. Franzmann, Martin J. Heinecken, William H. Narum, Warren A. Quanbeck, and Theodore G. Tappert. Alternates to this first dialogue were Paul M.

Bretscher, Harold Ditmanson, William H. Lazareth, and Fred W. Meuser.

We have also been informed by the theological work which resulted a decade later in the Leuenberg Agreement between Lutheran and Reformed churches in Europe. This Agreement officially reports that the churches did:

> affirm together the common understanding of the gospel. . . . This common understanding of the gospel enables them to declare and to realize church fellowship.
>
> It follows that agreement on the right teaching of the gospel and the right administration of the sacraments is the necessary and sufficient prerequisite for the true unity of the church. It is from these Reformation criteria that the participating churches derive their view of church fellowship as set out below.[4]

In our present discussions with the Reformed participants and our examination of their Confessions and liturgies, we have invoked the same fundamental criteria as posed by our Lutheran colleagues in dialogue with the Episcopal Church:

> Are we able mutually to affirm the presence of the gospel and apostolicity in our respective communions sufficiently to agree that the renewal of the church is more likely to come in communion with one another than out of communion with one another?[5]

By convention action in 1982 our churches recognized: "the Episcopal Church as a church in which the Gospel is preached and taught."[6]

On similar grounds we are persuaded that Lutheran churches should recognize the presence of the gospel in those churches which affirm the Reformed Confessions and make them a living part of their present witness and proclamation. We believe that this official declaration should be made by our churches at the earliest appropriate time at the highest level.

We are also persuaded that Lutheran churches should recognize the ordained ministry of word and sacrament of those churches and that this declaration should be made by our churches at the earliest appropriate time at the highest level.

We are also persuaded that Lutheran churches should, at the earliest appropriate time and at the highest level, officially recognize the Eucharists (Lord's Suppers) of those churches which affirm the Reformed Confessions and have them as a living part of their present witness and proclamation.

We make these recommendations because we have learned and now report:

1. Lutheran churches and many churches of the Reformed tradition are confessional churches. This permits, for instance, immediate comparison of doctrine between our churches and the Presbyterian Church (U.S.A.) and the Reformed Church in America. We have been able to consult clear, normative statements, interpreted by hermeneutics similar to those used by ourselves.[7]

We note that the styles of these several Confessions are somewhat different and that these styles reflect their different historical settings. The CA shows Reformation churches relating to the catholic tradition. Much of it is doxological in tone. The Reformed Confessions, like our own FC, are written a generation later. They assume the break with Rome, and they seek to mark out an identity for new churches in a new context.[8]

But the difference in style and setting and the address of different problems must never obscure the fact that Calvin knew and on several occasions was positive about the CA and that both Lutheran and Reformed Confessions speak with one voice on justification and the gospel.

2. Our churches are one in their confessional testimony on justification by grace through faith. Indeed we have found basic unanimity on this article beginning with Calvin's *Institutes* and the WC through the first two Lutheran-Reformed dialogues and the Leuenberg Agreement a decade ago.

The univocal affirmation of this article "on which the church stands or falls" would seem to require our churches' public response to those churches which make that confession.

3. We identified no church-dividing problems in our consideration of the ministry of the whole people of God or of the ordained ministry of word and sacrament.

We did hear language and terminology which is strange to Lutheran ears, for example, teaching elder, ruling elder, doctors, and deacons. But we agreed that the ministry functioning under these terms is congruent with the ministry as we have known it in our own churches in North America.

We agree that there is no issue here between the Lutheran and the Reformed traditions, or in the practice of our churches in North America, on the matter identified as "the validity of orders."

It is possible that Lutherans might learn from the Reformed tradition the value of a carefully structured body of elders in the theological as well as the business decisions of congregations, presbyteries, classes, and synods and of prominent lay participation in the functions of *episkopē*.

4. We identified no church-dividing issues of polity.

We found, again, language and terminology that sounded strange (and sometimes initially offensive) to Lutheran ears. But what the Reformed call governance, Lutherans call polity; what is contained in the "law for the presbytery" or a book of order is what Lutherans experience in constitutions, bylaws, and standards. A Presbyterian session or a Reformed consistory may be understood as in many ways functionally equivalent to a Lutheran church council. The Reformed practice of putting responsibility for instruction on parents and sponsors at baptism, as well as of deciding first admission to the Lord's Table by the session, is an interesting illustration of distributing ministerial responsibilities beyond the ordained ministry of word and sacrament.

While the language may be different, Lutherans should recognize that they have lived in the United States for over two centuries under a modified presbyterial polity.

In reference to the current ecumenical discussion of the "historic episcopate," Lutherans have consistently insisted that the only thing necessary (*satis est*) for the true unity of the church is agreement in the gospel and the sacraments. As we are faithful to that confessional principle, diverse forms of polity need not become church dividing. That principle permits, for instance, the Church of Sweden to recognize the apostolicity and validity of the ordained ministry of word and sacraments in all churches of the Lutheran Confessions. There is no confessional reason why this matter should affect our relationships with churches of the Reformed Confessions.

It is possible that Lutherans could learn from the Reformed model of what might be called a "collegial episcopate." In this model we may identify in the presbytery or classis an alternative to the historic monarchical episcopate. In presbytery or classis elders and ministers of the word and sacrament collectively exercise functions of *episkopē* (oversight) in a carefully constructed democratic model. Indeed, much of what Lutherans often perceive as obsessive Reformed preoccupation with order and structure functions precisely to assure shared and meaningful participation of elders as well as ministers of word and sacrament in decisions that will seem good to the Holy Spirit and to the people of God.

We urge affirmative action by our churches on the recommendations of this dialogue because we have also examined two issues that have had an abrasive history between Lutherans and Reformed in their theological reflections:

1. Lutheran theologians have from time to time criticized the Reformed affirmation of what has been called "the third use of the law." We do not perceive this to be a confessional issue, but rather a difference of theological reflection as much among Lutherans as between Lutherans and Reformed. We do not believe that Lutherans should ask of the Reformed agreement on a matter where there is no consistency in Lutheran teaching.

While it is clear that there is a difference in emphasis on this point between the traditions, we read the Formula of Concord[9] as affirming the parameters of acceptable Lutheran posture. We see no sense in which the Reformed Confessions obscure the gospel in their emphasis on this matter.

2. Lutherans and Reformed have traditionally polemicized over the mode of Christ's presence in the Eucharist. In this dialogue we are persuaded that these differences of interpretation have lost their church-dividing character. There is common doctrinal agreement among our historic Confessions, Lutheran-Reformed Dialogue I (*Marburg Revisited*), Lutheran-Reformed Dialogue II, and the Leuenberg Agreement that:[10]

a. The Lord's Supper is a sacrament.

b. The Lord's Supper is a means of grace.

c. In the Lord's Supper the true body and blood are present and are eaten and drunk.

d. The Lord's Supper is understood in the light of the saving act of God in Christ.

e. The same gift is offered in preached word and administered Sacrament.

f. The Sacrament is a form of visible, enacted word through which Christ and his saving benefits are effectively offered to men [i.e., persons].

g. The Sacrament does not simply serve to confirm a faith that is awakened by preaching; it also arouses faith through its presentation of the gospel.

h. The presence of Christ in the Sacrament is not effected by faith, but acknowledged by faith.

i. In the Lord's Supper the risen Christ imparts himself in his body and blood given up for all, through his word of promise with bread and wine. He thereby grants us forgiveness of sins and sets us free for a new life of faith.

j. We cannot separate communion with Jesus Christ and his body and blood from the act of eating and drinking. To be concerned about the manner of Christ's presence in the Lord's Supper in abstraction from this act is to run the risk of obscuring the meaning of the Lord's Supper.

Lutherans must learn that those churches that have subscribed to the Reformed Confessions have always taught and still teach the real presence of Christ in the Eucharist. Polemics often incorrectly ascribe to Reformed confessional doctrine an understanding of the Supper as simply a memorial to an absent Christ. Calvin taught a very high view of the Sacrament, described its benefits in language clearly reminiscent of Luther, and urged weekly communion. The Presbyterian Church (U.S.A.) today urges similar weekly frequency. The actual frequency today in both Reformed and Lutheran churches falls too short of that norm which we both share.[11]

In this dialogue we have had fruitful opportunity to reflect on this issue not simply in the language of the historic Confessions, but also in the language of *Baptism, Eucharist and Ministry*.

While our churches have not yet had the opportunity to respond officially to this text, both Lutheran and Reformed participants in this dialogue have experienced mutual appreciation of its biblical foundations and its attempt to bridge and transcend past differences.

The reader of our Joint Statement on the Sacrament of the Lord's Supper will note that the language of *BEM* is explicitly used. Both Lutheran and Reformed participants in this dialogue affirm: "It is in virtue of the living word of Christ and the power of the Holy Spirit that the bread and wine become the sacramental signs of Christ's body and blood."[12] "In the history of the Church there have been various attempts to understand the mystery of the real and unique presence of Christ in the Eucharist. Some are content merely to affirm this presence without seeking to explain it."[13]

We find that the Reformed members of this dialogue speak of their *experience* of the Supper in a way quite congruent with the testimony of Lutherans of their *experience* of the presence of Christ in the Sacrament.

It was important for us to return to words written by Warren Quanbeck two decades ago, for he anticipated this posture of convergence and mutual appreciation of traditions:

The historical study of the scriptures and of the development of eucharistic doctrine has shown how rich and complex the Christian tradition is at this point. Each of the great traditions has developed one aspect of the biblical witness and worked out its implications for the whole of Christian doctrine, for worship, and for service. Other elements have not usually been excluded, but have not been worked out with the same thoroughness. When the traditions are set alongside each other and examined in a sympathetic way, it can be seen that one does not necessarily have to choose one doctrinal tradition to the exclusion of all others. *To be a loyal Lutheran does not mean that one can see no value in the dogmatic or liturgical tradition of the Eastern Orthodox churches, or that one must condemn the total doctrinal statement of the Roman Catholic or Calvinist traditions.* The New Testament witnesses to a rich variety of theological motifs in interpreting the Lord's Supper: memorial, communion, thanksgiving, sacrifice, mystery, anticipation. *No tradition in the church has done justice to them all;* . . . Here one can see how Thomas Aquinas and John Calvin strive to assert the same religious concerns, *how Luther's profound sacramental realism can be complemented by Calvin's stress on the Holy Spirit.* . . .[14]

There is no question that there has been and still remains a difference in understanding between Lutheran and Reformed doctrine on the *mode* of Christ's real presence in the Sacrament. This is documented in note 4 of our Joint Statement on the Sacrament of the Lord's Supper. But we read *both* traditions as trying to "protect and preserve the dynamic of authentic sacramental union between Christ, the believer, and the other faithful over against the opposing extremes of mere symbolic recollection and the magic of transubstantiation."[15]

This is not the only dialogue between confessional families where the issue of language and style of explanation of the presence has surfaced. Lutherans have been challenged to reexamine their traditional insistence that the experience of the presence of the living Lord in the Supper be expressed by other faith communities in our language.

One such case would be Lutherans and Catholics in Dialogue III, which struggles with this very issue in language strongly reminiscent of Lutheran conversations with the Reformed.

Through the centuries Christians have attempted various formulations to describe this presence. Our confessional documents have in common affirmed that Jesus Christ is "really," "truly," and "substantially" present in this sacrament. This manner of presence "we can scarcely express in words," but we affirm his presence because we believe in the power of God and the promise of Jesus Christ, "This is my body. . . . This is my blood . . ." Our traditions have spoken of this presence as "sacramental," "supernatural" and "spiritual." These terms have different connotations in the two traditions, but they have in common a rejection of a spatial or natural manner of presence, and a rejection of an understanding of the sacrament as only commemorative or figurative. The term "sign," once suspect, is again recognized as a positive term for speaking of Christ's presence in the sacrament. For, though symbols and symbolic actions are used, the Lord's supper is an effective sign: it communicates what it promises; ". . . the action of the Church becomes the effective means whereby God in Christ acts and Christ is present with his people."[16]

In this present dialogue we must recall that Lutheran participants in the Lutheran-Episcopal Dialogue II made historic decisions about unity. They agreed that the *satis est* (it is sufficient) has been satisfied when it is recognized that the gospel is actually preached and the sacraments administered so they communicate the gospel. *It is not necessary, they affirmed, to have complete agreement in doctrinal statements about the gospel and the sacraments.*[17]

Indeed LED II noted that doctrinal areas requiring "further examination in future dialogues would laudably include: (1) the theology of the consecration and its practical consequences in regard to the elements; (2) the pastoral concern in administration (open and closed communion); (3) further clarification of the doctrine of the Real Presence; (4) the concept of 'sacrifice' in the Eucharist; (5) the relation of the Eucharist to the historic episcopate."[18] We see no such range of still unresolved issues with churches that subscribe to the Reformed Confessions.

Lutherans, of course, will notice a different liturgical style when they commune in a congregation of the Reformed tradition. Styles of music are often quite different. But the structures of the eucharistic liturgies of the Presbyterian Church (U.S.A.) and the Reformed Church in America are identical to that of the *Lutheran Book of Worship*.[19]

We must remember that immediately following the *satis est* clause of Augsburg Confession 7 is written the following sentence: "It is not necessary for the true unity of the Christian church that ceremonies instituted by men should be observed uniformly in all places." That is as much a confessional statement as the *satis est* clause.

We understand the recommendations for action which we transmit to our churches to be recommendations for expressing unity. They do not propose organic union among churches of the Reformed and Lutheran Confessions. They set out a process of reconciliation.

We affirm that Lutherans should celebrate their heritage and the Reformed theirs. Churches of the Lutheran and Reformed Confessions are not identical in style, in ethos, or in experienced history. Nonetheless we are called to witness to that unity in Christ which reconciles and challenges our diversities. For we share a common gospel, common sacraments, a common setting for proclamation and mission. We struggle against the same "principalities and powers."

We believe that Christ now calls us to common Eucharist and common mission. The commonality between churches which affirm and live under the Lutheran and Reformed Confessions has been identified in gospel, sacraments, and ministry.

The Lutheran World Federation Report, *The Unity of the Church: Requirements and Structure*, suggests four criteria to be met in the reconciling process: (1) "agreement in respect of the 'center of the Christian faith' "; (2) "recognition of the distinctiveness of the other confession 'as a legitimate form of Christian existence' and therefore no longer a divisive difference to be condemned"; (3) "fellowship in baptism and eucharist and the mutual recognition of ministries"; and (4) "'the binding common purpose of witness and service.' "[20]

In the perspective of these criteria, the time has then come, and the challenge before the churches is, to express this theological reality in eucharistic and pulpit hospitality and acts of common mission.

We understand this reconciling process to be dynamic and moving toward God's future. It must include living encounter, continuing theological dialogue, and mutual correction.

For our part we see no theological or contextual reasons that now would be impediments to eucharistic and pulpit hospitality and common mission. It may be identified by others; we would recommend that any further official conversations be scheduled in this new context of the reconciling process.

We are convinced that the force of the CA lays the burden of proof on those who would resist unity when there is agreement in the gospel.

We heartily recommend to the churches An Invitation to Action, and we encourage the earliest positive response at the highest level in each of our Lutheran churches.

## NOTES

1. Only The Lutheran Church—Missouri Synod did officially receive this report. Lack of Lutheran response and action should perhaps be understood in the context of the most important ecumenical agenda for Lutherans during the 1960s, the search for unity and possible union of all Lutheran bodies in this country.

2. Eleventh Biennial Convention, Lutheran Church in America, September 1982, p. 266 of the *Minutes*. Delegate Assembly, Association of Evan-

gelical Lutheran Churches, 7–9 September 1982, pp. 30–32 of the Proceedings. General Convention of The American Lutheran Church, September 1982, Reports and Actions, Part III of the Proceedings (Action #GC82.9.45).

3. *Marburg Revisited*, ed. Paul C. Empie and James I. McCord (Minneapolis: Augsburg Publishing House, 1966), p. 2 of the Preface, italics added. Criticisms of *Marburg Revisited* are to be found in *Lutherans in Ecumenical Dialogue: An Interpretative Guide* (New York: LCUSA, 1977), pp. 10–11. The criticisms must be taken seriously but perhaps are best understood in light of further analysis of the Lutheran-Reformed dialogues found in the following note.

4. Cf. Appendix 3 for the complete text of the Leuenberg Agreement. For an analysis and evaluation of the Leuenberg Agreement see *Ecumenical Relations of the Lutheran World Federation: Report of the Working Group on the Interrelations Between the Various Bilateral Dialogues* (Geneva: LWF, 1977), passim, carried out by a committee led by Robert J. Marshall. Important in this evaluation is the fact that criticisms are often based more on the method used, such as using documentation or not, rather than on the substance of the dialogue itself. Note especially the two paragraphs cited in this footnote:

> (87) The LA, for its part, insists firmly on the christological prerequisite of Christ's self-emptying by means of his incarnation and draws the necessary conclusions from this for the doctrine of the Lord's Supper (*finitum capax infiniti*). The following affirmation is made: "In the word of the promise and in the sacraments, the Holy Spirit, and so God himself, makes the crucified and risen Jesus present to us" (No. 21). This sentence also puts into words a concrete expression of pneumatology which links the work of the Holy Spirit with bodily presence. The Lutheran tradition itself referred in this sentence to a "spiritual presence" in the Lord's Supper (Form. Conc. SD VII: 105) although this expression is not used in the LA. This gives even stronger emphasis to the Lutheran view of the bodily presence. The assessment of the bread and wine in the Lord's Supper as the means of the presence of Christ is thereby guaranteed. The natural consequences of this are the recognition of the *manducatio oralis* and of the *manducatio indignorum*.

> (91) Whereas one could—in the sense just touched upon—wish that the involvement of Lutherans in different dialogues should open up new avenues in Eucharistic thinking, one must remember the following: Lutherans carry on dialogues with different partners and each of them are [*sic*] in their turn in dialogue with other traditions. While one may miss certain traditional questions of the Lutheran tradition in the dialogues in which we are involved, many of these points have been discussed by our partners in other dialogues. Thus the Reformed are in the process of dialogue with the Roman Catholic Church. There they deal with

the Eucharist as the place of Christ's presence. Certain aspects of that dialogue may make clear points missed in the LA. A similar case is also found in the regional Swiss dialogue, where the Reformed have elaborated a rich Eucharistic doctrine with the Catholics. [See: *Für ein gemeinsames eucharistisches Zeugnis der Kirchen. Arbeitsdokument der Ökumenischen Gesprächskommission der Schweiz,* 1973.] Such observations might balance the relative brevity of the LA and answer questions which the Lutheran tradition may raise. This corresponds to the nature of the matter. The purpose of bilateral dialogues is not intended to produce a comprehensive treatment of all subjects but progress towards practical, bilateral clarification in each case.

Further discussion among those holding the Leuenberg Agreement has concerned the doctrine of the two kingdoms, the office of the ministry, and the nature of fellowship; see Andre Birmele, ed., *Konkordie und Kirchengemeinschaft reformatorisher Kirchen im Europa der Gegenwart. Texte der Konferenz von Driebergen*, Ökumenische Perspectiven 10 (Frankfurt am Main: Verlag Otto Lembeck and Verlag Josef Knecht, 1982).

5. *Lutheran-Episcopal Dialogue, A Progress Report* (Cincinnati: Forward Movement Publications, 1972). This is the Report of Lutheran-Episcopal Dialogue I in the United States, concluded in 1972.

6. See n. 2.

7. Lutherans often do not recognize the force of Confessions in the life of many churches of the Reformed tradition.

Illustrative of confessional statement is:

a. The *BO* of the PC(U.S.A.), which includes: the Nicene Creed, the Apostles' Creed, the Scots Confession, the Heidelberg Catechism, the Second Helvetic Confession, the Westminster Confession of Faith, the Larger Catechism, the Shorter Catechism, the Theological Declaration of Barmen, the Confession of 1967 (*BO* G–1.0501)

b. The constitutional statement of the force of these Confessions in the life and practice of this church:

> In these confessional statements the church declares to its members and to the world who and what it is, what it believes, what it resolves to do. These statements identify the church as a community of people known by its convictions as well as by its actions. They guide the church in its study and interpretation of the Scriptures; they summarize the essence of Christian tradition; they direct the church in maintaining sound doctrines; they equip the church for its work of proclamation. These confessional statements are subordinate standards in the church, subject to the authority of Jesus Christ, the Word of God, as the Scriptures bear witness to him. While confessional standards are subordinate to the Scriptures, they are, nonetheless, standards. They are not lightly drawn up or subscribed to, nor may they be ignored or dismissed. The church is prepared to counsel

with or even to discipline one ordained who seriously rejects the faith expressed in the confessions. . . . In its confessions, the PC(U.S.A.) gives witness to the faith of the church catholic. The confessions express the faith of the one, holy, catholic, and apostolic church in the recognition of canonical Scriptures and the formulation and adoption of the ecumenical creeds, notably the Nicene and Apostles' Creeds. . . . The Protestant watchwords—grace alone, faith alone, Scripture alone—embody principles of understanding which continue to guide and motivate the people of God in the life of faith. (PC[U.S.A.] *BO* G–2.0100–2.0400)

c. Among the questions asked of the candidate at the ordination of a minister of word and sacrament:

b. Do you accept the Scriptures of the Old and New Testament to be, by the Holy Spirit, the unique and authoritative witness to Jesus Christ in the church universal, and God's Word to you?; c. Do you sincerely receive and adopt the essential tenets of the Reformed faith as expressed in the confessions of our church as authentic and reliable expositions of what Scripture leads us to believe and do, and will you be instructed and led by those confessions as you lead the people of God? d. Will you be a minister of the Word in obedience to Jesus Christ, under the authority of Scripture, and continually guided by our confessions? (PC[U.S.A.] *BO* G–14.0405)

The situation of the UCC is somewhat different. This church is a product of the merger of the Congregational Christian Churches and the Evangelical Reformed Church in 1957.

The parallel constitutional material on confessional commitment of the UCC is:

The United Church of Christ acknowledges as its sole Head, Jesus Christ, Son of God and Saviour. It acknowledges as kindred in Christ all who share this confession. It looks to the Word of God in the Scriptures, and to the presence and power of the Holy Spirit, to prosper its creative and redemptive work in the world. It claims as its own the faith of the historic Church expressed in the ancient creeds and reclaimed in the basic insights of the Protestant Reformers. It affirms the responsibility of the Church in each generation to make this faith its own in reality of worship, in honesty of thought and expression, and in purity of heart before God. In accordance with the teachings of our Lord and the practice prevailing among evangelical Christians, it recognizes two sacraments: Baptism and the Lord's Supper or Holy Communion. (*Constitution and Bylaws,* Preamble 2)

Among the questions asked of UCC candidates at the ordination of ministers of word and sacrament are:

Do you, with the Church throughout the world, hear the Word of

> God in the Scriptures of the Old and New Testaments, and do you accept it as the rule of Christian faith and practice?
>
> Will you be zealous in maintaining both the truth of the gospel and the peace of the Church, speaking the truth in love?
>
> Do you accept the faith and order of the United Church of Christ; and will you, as an ordained minister in this communion, show compassionate affection toward all who are in Christ? (*A Manual on the Ministry* [New York: Office for Church Life and Leadership, UCC, 1977], p. 66)

We found the representative of the United Church of Christ at this dialogue, Dr. Frederick H. Herzog, personally and persistently speaking of the gospel, justification, and the Lord's Supper in unmistakably Lutheran language. This would be true of many individuals in this church.

But we feel it is important for the integrity of this dialogue for us to report these differences in the degrees of official confessional commitment among the churches of the Reformed tradition which were represented in this dialogue.

8. Warren A. Quanbeck, "Confessional Integrity and Ecumenical Dialogue," *Marburg Revisited*, pp. 184–190, or pp. 45–52 of this volume.

9. FC, Epitome, 4, 18, *BkC* 477; 5, 11, *BkC* 479; 6, *BkC* 479–81; FC SD, 6, esp. 25b, *BkC* 563–68.

10. Cf. the complete texts for the summary statements, *Marburg Revisited*, Appendix 1; for the sections on the Lord's Supper, Leuenberg Agreement, Appendix 3. The results of the Lutheran-Reformed Dialogue II were not published, but see Appendix 2.

Quotations a, b, and c are agreements reached in Lutheran-Reformed Dialogue II; quotations d, e, f, g, and h were agreements reached at Lutheran-Reformed Dialogue I (*Marburg Revisited*, pp. 103–4); quotations i and j are statement nos. 15 and 19 in the Leuenberg Agreement.

11. E.g., a memorandum from the Division for Parish Services, LCA, dated June 1983, reported that only 14.7 percent of congregations in that church had reported weekly frequency of the Eucharist in 1982.

12. *BEM*, pp. 13 and 15.

13. *BEM*, pp. 13–15.

14. Quanbeck, "Confessional Integrity" pp. 189–90, italics added, or p. 51 of this volume.

15. Cf. our Joint Statement on the Sacrament of the Lord's Supper, n. 4. The most recent theological reflection on the issue of presence is made by Carl Braaten in his *Principles of Lutheran Theology* (Philadelphia: Fortress Press, 1983), pp. 94–95:

> Although the sixteenth century ended with sharp controversies between the Lutherans and the Reformed on Christology and the Lord's Supper, driving a wedge between the two branches of the Reformation that would last for centuries, there are many healthy signs of ecumenical rapprochement in the twentieth century. Cer-

tainly we have passed beyond trench warfare into peace negotiations, as evidenced in the Leuenberg Agreement between Lutherans and Reformed in Germany. The pivotal argument between Zwingli and Luther tended to eclipse many dimensions of the Lord's Supper that have been rediscovered through biblical, patristic, liturgical, and ecumenical studies, providing a broader area of common ground than was previously thought possible. Rigid stereotypes can be broken down and new results can be expected, although they do not automatically clear away old differences that may still have far-reaching effects on worship life in our various communities. We should also remember that what panels of theologians may accomplish at the level of bilateral dialogues seldom has more than a ripple effect on the actual liturgical practice of congregations. Yet there is reason for optimism that the antithesis between the Reformed and Luther's followers can be softened, if not fully overcome.

There has been in fact a recovery of greater sacramental realism among Reformed theologians. In Germany during World War II, Christians faced an emergency situation, and in their suffering they often shared the same table of the Lord. This real fellowship in Christ has been continued and expanded in the meantime. Other factors have also played a role. There has arisen the historical-critical approach to the Bible with negative effects on the way Lutherans have traditionally argued their position on the Lord's Supper. Luther research has shown that there were real differences between Luther, Melanchthon, Chemnitz and other confessional theologians, and that these theologians by no means represent a monolithic doctrine. The ecumenical movement has opened lines of access to the traditions of Eastern Orthodoxy, widening the arena in which eucharistic theology may be developed and overcoming the frozen positions between the rival parties in Western Christianity. Altar and pulpit fellowship has been practiced between Lutherans and Reformed, convincing many believers that the Lord's Supper controversy need no longer divide the communions.

The critical study of the Scriptures has made it clear that neither Luther nor the Lutheran tradition grasped the *totality* of the biblical witness to the Lord's Supper.

16. Paul C. Empie and T. Austin Murphy, eds., *The Eucharist as Sacrifice*, Lutherans and Catholics in Dialogue III (New York: U.S.A. National Committee of the LWF and Bishops' Committee for Ecumenical and Interreligious Affairs, 1967), pp. 192–93.

17. *Lutheran-Episcopal Dialogue. Report and Recommendations* (Cincinnati: Forward Movement Publications, 1981); cf. the entire section on "The Theological Methodology of LED II," pp. 13–22, especially the paragraphs on justification (pp. 14–15) and the Eucharist (pp. 16–18). We call attention to these remarks:

> Both communions affirm the real presence of Christ's Body and Blood in the Lord's Supper, but they express this faith somewhat differently. (p. 16)
>
> In most contemporary exegesis the words "body" and "blood" are interpreted increasingly not as substances but as saving event (*Heilsereignis*). (p. 17)
>
> To some Lutherans it may seem strange that limited agreement on controverted dogmatic *loci* should be thought adequate for some degree of ecclesial relationship, when the classical Lutheran position has been that the complete confessional agreement is essential for union. However, Dr. Rusch reports some change here in some recent Lutheran thinking. . . . Here there is recognition for the first time of the possibility of multiple expressions of doctrine. A model of church unity for much of recent Lutheran theology is that of a fellowship in which confessional peculiarities are not blended but reconciled as legitimate pluralism. In such a pattern joint statements would represent an essential core of dogmatic agreement within a wider pluralism. (pp. 19–20)

Representatives of LCMS dissented from this understanding of *satis est*.

18. Ibid., p. 29, n. 3.

19. The "difference" between Reformed and Lutheran eucharistic liturgies may be more in the use of musical settings by the Lutherans than in the texts. For instance, the *structure of the eucharistic liturgy of the Presbyterian Church (U.S.A.) is identical to that of the LBW:* there is a confession and declaration of pardon (p. 25) (this is not optional, as in the *LBW*); it is assumed that the Service for the Lord's Day includes the Lord's Supper, but option is given to conclude the service without the Supper (p. 34); gifts of bread and wine are presented at the table (p. 34); the *sursum corda* and preface are spoken (p. 34); there is a threefold eucharistic prayer which is trinitarian, containing the words of institution and an epiklesis (pp. 35–36); the use of wine is explicitly directed in a rubric (pp. 36–37); there is a post-communion canticle (p. 37). Cf. *Worshipbook* (Philadelphia: Westminster Press, 1972). Similar congruence in eucharistic liturgy is found in the Reformed Church in America.

20. Günther Gassmann and Harding Meyer, *The Unity of the Church*, LWF Report 15 (Stuttgart: LWF, 1983), p. 14.

# FROM THE REFORMED DELEGATION TO THE REFORMED FAMILY OF CHURCHES

We who have represented your churches in the third round of Lutheran-Reformed dialogue have been grateful for the opportunity to come to know our Lutheran colleagues, their concerns, their special history in America, their warmth toward their Reformed "cousins," and above all their deep Christian faith. Our lives have been touched, our faith enriched, and our experiences broadened by this two-year dialogue. It is our profound hope that our work will open new opportunities for you, too, to enter into such an experience of Reformed-Lutheran fellowship, mutual enrichment in the faith, and partnership in the church's mission.

Our report represents an urgent appeal that this renewal of dialogue result in new partnership in mission and thus in new expressions of our unity in Christ. We believe it is now appropriate for our churches officially to allow and encourage our ministers to stand in one another's place in worship and the sacraments and for congregations to enter into fellowship at the Lord's Table. Since such official action is usually described in ecumenical dialogue as "mutual recognition" of churches, that language has been used in our report, though it is not language to which our Reformed churches have become accustomed. We recognize in one another authentic churches of Jesus Christ and desire full expression in our church life of that mutual recognition. For such new partnership to come into being, action is required by the governing bodies of our churches at all levels.

What are we asking of the Reformed churches which we represent?

I. Steps which we believe could be taken immediately on the basis of existing commitments:

(a) We ask that our report be studied at the national level by theological and ecumenical commissions and the General Assemblies and General Synods, at the level of presbytery, conference, and classis, and locally by pastors, elders, and deacons as well as other members of congregations. In the many communities where both Lutheran and Reformed congregations can be found, it is our hope that Reformed people will invite neighboring Lutheran congregations to study the report with them as a means of becoming acquainted. We urge further that the communities of our theological institutions make the study of this document a priority.

(b) Reformed people need to be reminded that it is already the policy of our churches that baptized Christians from other traditions, including Lutherans, are welcome to participate in the Lord's Supper in our churches. It is also our practice to invite ministers of certain other Christian traditions, including Lutherans, to participate in preaching and sacramental observances and even to become members of presbyteries, classes, or conferences where they are called to serve in ministries in which our churches participate. The fact that this possibility already exists has not in fact often resulted in the development of strong ties of fellowship between Reformed and Lutheran congregations in the same communities. Despite the closeness of our historic ties in the sixteenth-century Reformation and the strong similarities in our confessional stances, a distance has grown up between us which leaves us somewhat ill at ease with each other. We are asking that Reformed congregations take the initiative to open doors to fellowship with Lutheran congregations, encouraging a new climate of hospitality and collegiality in the work of Christ's church.

(c) We request our General Synods and General Assemblies after study to take prompt and effective action to implement the recommendations of An Invitation to Action on pp. 4–6. These recommendations for Reformed churches commend reaffirmation of Lutheran ministries. Approval of our recommendations could represent a new commitment to engage our churches in common mission outreach to the world, common study, and common worship at every judicatory level, to the fullest extent that the Lutheran churches' action will make possible.

We understand that acceptance of our recommendations would begin to shape a future of closer collaboration as heirs of the Reformation, engaged in proclamation of the gospel to our contemporaries and committed to ongoing reformation of the church so that that task can be more joyfully and effectively accomplished.

II. Steps which might eventually be considered as relationships deepen:

(a) Our churches could revise their books of order where necessary to make it possible for Lutheran pastors seeking to join our presbyteries, classes, or associations to be received in the same way as pastors coming from other Reformed churches. This step would acknowledge that our churches belong to the larger Reformation tradition and already are parts of the same branch of the Christian family from the standpoint of both theology and polity.

(b) Our churches might also consider adding the Augsburg Confession to our books of Confessions as a recognition of the debt the Reformed tradition owes to the Lutheran one theologically. We remember that the United Church of Christ is already rooted in the tradition of the Augsburg Confession through its heritage from the Evangelical and Reformed Church.

We commend our report to the churches we represent with our prayers that the Holy Spirit may use this process of study and reception to bring new understanding and new life to all our churches and with our happy anticipation that our churches will find new joy in their unity in our common Lord, Jesus Christ.